A SHORT HISTORY OF
WORLD
WAR II

D1340921

A SHORT HISTORY OF
WORLD WAR II

Nigel Cawthorne

with

Karen Farrington and Paul Roland

ARCTURUS

ARCTURUS

This edition published in 2013 by Arcturus Publishing Limited
26/27 Bickels Yard, 151–153 Bermondsey Street,
London SE1 3HA

ISBN: 978-1-78212-280-7
AD003630EN

Printed in Malaysia

Contents

INTRODUCTION **6**

CHAPTER 1 THE ROAD TO WAR **8**

CHAPTER 2 WAR IN EUROPE **17**

CHAPTER 3 WAR IN THE DESERT **35**

CHAPTER 4 THE RUSSIAN FRONT **50**

CHAPTER 5 WAR IN THE PACIFIC **65**

CHAPTER 6 THE SOFT UNDERBELLY **77**

CHAPTER 7 THE LIBERATION OF FRANCE **88**

CHAPTER 8 THE MARCH ON GERMANY **104**

CHAPTER 9 INTO THE REICH **118**

CHAPTER 10 THE FAR EAST **136**

CHAPTER 11 BURMA **149**

CHAPTER 12 ISLAND HOPPING **159**

CHAPTER 13 ENDGAME **178**

INDEX **190**

World War II was the central event of the twentieth century. While World War I – the Great War or the 'war to end all wars' – can hardly be considered a mere curtain-raiser, it was largely confined to Europe and the Middle East. World War II also engulfed Asia and the Pacific.

The origins of World War II lay in World War I. During the war, military reverses caused a revolution that brought down the Tsarist monarchy and installed a Communist government in Russia which, by 1922, was in the hands of Joseph Stalin. The fall of the monarchies in Vienna and Berlin made way for weak democratic governments that were easily overthrown.

Italy had been an ally of Britain, France and, latterly, the US in World War I. Although a victor, it felt cheated by the post-war settlement. The resulting economic crisis caused political instability, resulting in the rise of a Fascist dictator, Benito Mussolini, in 1922. Then Adolf Hitler, an Austrian war veteran leading a small party in Bavaria, took Mussolini as his model.

Like many in Germany, Hitler did not feel that they had lost the war. Indeed, the fighting was brought to an end on 11 November 1918 by an armistice. However, at the peace conference held at Versailles the following year, a peace treaty was forced on Germany which limited its armed forces to those of a minor power, levied reparations that resulted in economic collapse and political chaos, and stripped Germany of its colonies and shrank its borders, which left hundreds of thousands of ethnic Germans in the surrounding countries who still felt an allegiance to Berlin.

Japan had also been an ally of Britain, France and America in World War I. Though it took little part in the fighting, supplying its allies led to a boom and, by the end of the war, Japan emerged as a great military and industrial power. However, at the Versailles Conference, the Japanese were denied the racial equality clause they wanted and were given only half of the German colonies in the Far East and the Pacific that they thought they were due. Their delegation walked out.

However, the German concession at Shandong, which was given to Japan rather than returned to China, was soon a cause of conflict. Japan then saw expansion on the mainland of Asia as the cure for the post-war slump and the militarists took over. With Fascist governments in power in Germany and Italy, the sides were drawn up for the largest and most devastating military conflict the world has ever seen.

World War I had also provided the combatants with new weapons – notably tanks and military aircraft. These demanded new tactics that made warfare fast and fluid. War was now an industrial process. It no longer solely involved vast armies confronting each other in pitched battles or across fixed lines. That meant that civilians became involved to a greater extent than before. The factory workers who made the weapons, and their families, were now a target to be killed, maimed, terrorized and made homeless.

It is thought that some fifty-five million people perished in the war. There are no reliable estimates of how many were wounded or permanently disabled. The Soviet Union alone lost eighteen million dead, including civilians. Hitler's mad adventure cost Germany 4,280,000 dead with five million military wounded. China lost 1,310,000 military dead and 1,752,951 wounded. But the millions of civilians who died as a result of various battles, bombardments, sieges, massacres, famines and diseases caused by the war remain uncounted.

Japan lost 1,300,000 fighting men, with four million wounded, along with 672,000 civilian dead. Poland suffered 5,675,000 dead, losing around 20 per cent of its pre-war population. Russia and Yugoslavia lost around 10 per cent; Germany only slightly less. Then there were 5.7 million Jews murdered in the death camps.

Britain lost 357,116 dead, including 92,673 civilians, and 277,077 military wounded. In all, the British Commonwealth as a whole lost 466,045 dead and 475,047 wounded, while America lost 298,131 dead, including six thousand civilians and 671,801 wounded.

In Britain, around 30 per cent of homes were destroyed in the Blitz. France, Belgium, the Netherlands and Greece lost around 20 per cent of their housing, while Poland lost some 30 per cent of its build stock.

The US Strategic Bombing Survey found that 39 per cent of the homes had been destroyed in Germany's forty-nine largest cities. In Japan, 30 per cent of city dwellers lost their homes and possessions with the devastation of 40 per cent of the built-up areas of sixty-six Japanese cities.

In 1945 there were some twenty-one million refugees in Europe. Over half were people who had been taken from their homelands as forced labour. Five million Soviet prisoners of war and forced labourers trudged home eastwards, while over eight million Germans fled west, out of the Soviet zone of occupation.

During the war, India suffered a famine which was not helped by the diversion of food and shipping to supply Britain and its armed forces. And China suffered floods and epidemics, while most of its hospitals had been destroyed.

It is estimated that the war cost the belligerents over a trillion dollars. That does not include the damage to the economy caused by the slaughter of able-bodied men, the destruction of shops, factories and the infrastructure, or the contribution made by forced labour. And no one can put a monetary value on the suffering, misery and deprivation the war inflicted.

And its effect did not end there. World War II left Europe – indeed the world – divided, with both sides bristling with nuclear weapons and ballistic missiles developed during the fighting. This armed stand-off – the Cold War – lasted until the fall of the Berlin Wall in 1989 and German reunification in 1990.

In China, the Communists, who had spent World War II fighting the Japanese, took over in 1949. They are still in power now.

Nigel Cawthorne, Bloomsbury

The atomic bomb explodes over Hiroshima, 6 August 1945

Chapter 1

THE ROAD TO WAR

Three years after completing his political testament *Mein Kampf*, Adolf Hitler wrote a second, untitled volume which he withheld from publication. He realized that he could not afford to make others aware of his unshakable conviction that a second European war was not only inevitable but necessary. It was the only way to secure *Lebensraum* – 'living space' – for the German people.

'Every healthy, unspoiled nation... sees the acquisition of new territory not as something useful but as something natural... He who would ban this sort of contention from earth from all eternity might possibly do away with the struggle of man against man, but he would also do away with earth's highest force for evolution,' he wrote.

This was Hitler's thinking in 1928 and it remained the foundation stone of his foreign policy once he was in power. It was Germany's destiny to engage in a life and death struggle with the Slavonic nations to prove the superiority of the Aryan race. If Germany proved worthy the reward would not only be a vast expanse of rich arable land and an almost limitless supply of slave labour, but also the natural resources of the Crimea and Ukraine. These regions included the vast oil fields vital for sustaining a modern empire and its war machine.

According to an aide, Hitler had a 'pathological need for battle'. He once confided to his commanders that the 'need to strike' had always been a part of his nature and that the war, when it came, would be the same struggle he had once fought out within himself. He believed that war was the final aim of politics, giving the aggressor the opportunity to 'cleanse' the conquered land of the 'unfit and unworthy'.

According to an aide, Hitler (seen here at Nuremberg in 1928) had a 'pathological need for battle' and he once confided that the 'need to strike' had always been part of his nature. War was inevitable

Nazi-inspired art: three young men struggle to push iron-ore uphill in a labour camp. Everyone had to toe the line and pull together behind the war effort, or face the consequences

But in 1933 Hitler was in no position to prosecute a war in Europe. The German army numbered fewer than 100,000 men, the figure imposed by the Versailles Treaty ending World War I. Even Poland had double that number and France had a far superior force – recalling the sacrifices made in the 1914–18 war, this favoured a defensive strategy. They dug themselves in behind the Maginot Line, 87 miles (140 km) of forts and bunkers running parallel with the German border from Belgium to Switzerland. Besides, the Rhineland on Germany's western border had been closed to the German military as a buffer zone between France and Germany.

Hitler knew he would give the French an excuse to march into Germany if he rearmed in open defiance of the Versailles Treaty. So in October 1933 he demanded that the French and the British reduce their armaments, knowing full well that they would refuse. This gave him an excuse to withdraw his delegation from the Geneva disarmament conference and pull out of the League of Nations, forerunner of the United Nations.

Hitler's second stratagem was to sign a ten-year, non-aggression pact with Poland in January 1934. This drove a wedge between the Allies and gave the Poles a reason to postpone the modernization of their armed forces.

The coal-rich Saar region had been taken by the League of Nations in part payment for reparations but under the terms of the Versailles Treaty it was returned when its inhabitants voted for reunification. This gave Germany a rich source of fuel for its rearmament programme. In March of 1935 Hitler announced the formation of the Luftwaffe, the new German air force, under the command of Field Marshal Hermann Göring, and the introduction of conscription. Both measures were blatant violations of the treaty.

Hitler then asked the British if he could build up the German navy to no more than a third of the size of the British fleet. Incredibly, they agreed. The tenuous alliance of anti-German nations came apart at the seams when, in October 1935, Italian dictator Benito Mussolini invaded Ethiopia, demonstrating the impotence of the League of Nations.

At home, Hitler began his persecution of the Jews, whom he blamed for Germany's defeat in World War I and the Depression of the 1930s. Under the Nazis anti-Semitism became government policy. They enacted a series of laws designed to exclude Jews from German public life. Jews were banned from the civil service, education, universities, medicine and journalism. The 1935 Nuremberg laws deprived Jews of their citizenship and prevented them from marrying non-Jews.

The Four-Year Plan

In 1936 Hitler instigated the Four-Year Plan, which ensured that by 1940 all the elements would be in place for a full-scale war in Western Europe. The first step was to reduce Germany's dependence on the importation of oil, rubber and iron ore by producing synthetic fuel and rubber, and increasing Germany's stockpile of low-grade iron ore.

While the factories worked to rearm the Reich, the future pilots of Göring's Luftwaffe trained in secret, using gliders under the pretence of being part of the League of Air Sports. Old cavalry regiments were disbanded and the men were being familiarized with the rapid mobility and firepower of small armoured vehicles. Tanks would soon be rolling off the production lines. Their commanders were being trained to take part in a new, fast-moving mechanized form of warfare known as Blitzkrieg – or 'lightning war' – developed by General Heinz Guderian and other forward-looking officers.

Il Duce and Der Führer ride together through Munich in June 1940. The Spanish Civil War had brought them together and Hitler's audacious reoccupation of the Rhineland cemented their alliance

Reoccupying the Rhineland

Hitler's next step was to move troops into the Rhineland – 9,450 square miles (24,475 square kilometres) of German territory bordering Holland, Belgium and France. Under the Locarno Pact of 1925, it had been demilitarized. Hitler knew that if he could recover the Rhineland, which included the important city of Cologne, he would enhance his reputation at home. So on the morning of 7 March 1936 22,000 German troops marched into the demilitarized zone, to the cheers of the inhabitants who threw flowers.

A detachment of 2,000 troops continued across the bridges into Cologne, with secret orders to turn back if the French opposed the crossing. But not a single French soldier could be seen. Hitler's popularity soared. Meanwhile, Hitler sold coal and weapons to the Italians and they joined forces in the fight against Communism in the Spanish Civil War which lasted from July 1936 to March 1939.

Austria

Hitler's eyes then turned on Austria, where he had been born. Indeed, Hitler only became a German citizen in 1932, the year before he became Chancellor. In the early 1930s there were forty thousand Nazi party members active in Vienna. Fearing an armed rebellion, in March 1933, the Austrian Chancellor Engelbert Dollfuss banned the Nazi party. In July 1934 Hitler sent 150 SS troops across the border dressed in Austrian uniforms to storm the Viennese cabinet and kill Dollfuss. They managed to mobilize the Austrian army, who arrested the SS men.

Madrid, 1939: the Falangists celebrate victory, inspiring other European fascists to take up arms

Dollfuss was succeeded by his deputy Kurt von Schuschnigg. On 12 February 1938, Hitler summoned Schuschnigg to his Bavarian retreat at Berchtesgaden and demanded that he lift the ban on the Austrian Nazi party and appoint Nazis to key ministries. Schuschnigg was then forced to hold a plebiscite where the Austrian people could choose between independence and Anschluss – that is, union with Germany.

On 11 March 1938, the day before the vote, Schuschnigg learned that Hitler had issued orders to invade. He resigned, to be succeeded by the pro-Nazi Arthur Seyss-Inquart. The following morning the German Eighth Army streamed across the border and took Hitler's homeland without a shot. Hitler made a personal appearance in Linz, where he had been brought up, later that day.

An estimated 70,000 socialists and other 'enemies of the Reich' were rounded up and imprisoned. Even Schuschnigg was to spend seven years behind bars. He was lucky. Jews were dragged from their homes and businesses, and forced to scrub the pavements.

Czechmate

Three million Germans lived in the Sudetenland inside Czechoslovakia's western border. On 24 April, goaded by Hitler, the Nazi-sponsored Sudeten German Party led by Konrad Henlein demanded autonomy for the Sudeten Germans, knowing full well that the Czech president Edvard Benes would refuse. While Henlein's thugs started riots, Germany used this as an excuse to prepare for war. Hitler had set a date for the invasion of Czechoslovakia. It was 30 September.

On 15 September British prime minister Neville Chamberlain flew to Berchtesgaden in a last-ditch effort to seek a compromise. Hitler said, if the

Into the spider's web: Neville Chamberlain is welcomed to Berchtesgaden by Hitler and his chief interpreter Paul Schmidt. Chamberlain's policy of appeasement cost the Czechs dear

Allies could guarantee that the Czechs would hand the Sudetenland over, he would order his army to stand down and give his 'sacred oath' that he would respect Czech sovereignty.

Chamberlain returned to cheering crowds in London. Britain and France then forced the Czech government to hand over the Sudetenland. Chamberlain flew back to Germany on 22 September believing that he had appeased the dictator and that signing the agreement was a mere formality. Instead Hitler rejected the Anglo-French proposals for an orderly withdrawal of Czech troops and police and, instead, demanded that they do so immediately.

This was no bluff. Hitler was ready for war. The German army had swelled from seven divisions to 51, with five heavy armoured divisions and four light ones, while the German navy could boast a formidable fleet consisting of two battleships of 31,200 tons, two heavy cruisers, 17 destroyers and 47 submarines. The Luftwaffe now had 21 squadrons, manned by pilots who had gained experience during the Spanish Civil War, while the German armaments industry was increasing its output. Back in Britain Chamberlain spoke of a 'quarrel in a far-away country between peoples of whom we know nothing'.

On 30 September, Hitler met with the British and French premiers in Munich, where Mussolini presented Hitler's demands as his own proposals for peace. The Czechs must withdraw from the Sudetenland by 1 October, giving up its main fortifications and heavy industry in that area. In return the Allies would guarantee the new frontier. The Czechs had no say in the matter and the Allies told themselves that they had no choice but to sign the Munich Agreement.

While the Czech armed forces were prepared to fight, President Benes had lost all faith that Britain and France would be good to their word, and on 1 October the first German divisions marched unopposed into the Sudetenland.

Peace in Our Time

As a postscript Chamberlain pressed Hitler into signing a hastily-drawn statement affirming Anglo-German co-operation in the event of a future dispute. On his return to London he waved the scrap of paper in triumph. He had secured, he said,

'peace with honour' and 'peace in our time'. But Conservative MP Winston Churchill, who had been warning of the dangers of German rearmament to no avail for years, declared that it was only 'the beginning of the reckoning'.

Hitler cared little about what foreigners thought though. He stepped up his persecution of the Jews, expelling all Polish Jews from Germany. Herschel Grynszpan, the seventeen-year-old son of a deported couple, shot the German ambassador in Paris. Two days later on 9 November 1938, when the ambassador died, the Nazis launched an organized assault against Jewish shops, businesses and temples. Dozens of Jews were killed and thousands were arrested and sent to concentration camps. This became known as *Kristallnacht*, or the 'night of broken glass'. When Germany invaded France, Grynszpan was handed over. He disappeared in German custody sometime after 1943 and was declared dead in 1960.

In the early hours of 14 March 1939 Hitler received the new Czech President Emil Hácha at the Chancellery in Berlin and presented him with an ultimatum. He could invite the German army to quell the alleged disturbances in his country, making Czechoslovakia a German protectorate, or he could watch Prague being bombed into rubble by the Luftwaffe. After having a mild heart attack Hácha was forced to sign a declaration requesting Germany's 'protection' along with an order for the Czech army

German troops enter the Sudetenland, which was mostly populated by ethnic Germans

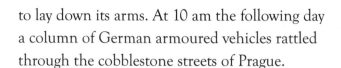

to lay down its arms. At 10 am the following day a column of German armoured vehicles rattled through the cobblestone streets of Prague.

Too Little, Too Late: the Fate of Poland

During the Czech crisis Poland's ruling military junta had been offered a share of the spoils provided they aligned themselves with Germany in the event of war. When they declined Hitler was hugely infuriated. Then he pressed them to join the Anti-Comintern Pact against Russia. Again they prevaricated.

In January 1939 Hitler's patience with the Poles was wearing thin. He received the Polish foreign minister, Colonel Josef Beck, at Berchtesgaden and repeated demands that Poland return the Baltic port of Danzig (Gdansk), made a free city by the Versailles Treaty, and allow Germany to build road and rail links through the Polish Corridor that divided Germany from East Prussia. Beck refused.

Britain and France had failed to come to the aid of democratic Czechoslovakia, but now declared themselves ready to go to war to support a military junta. Hitler reacted by promising the British 'a stew they will choke on'.

On 15 March German troops marched into Bohemia, Moravia and Slovakia – formerly parts of Czechoslovakia, fencing Poland in on three sides. On 3 April, Hitler issued a top secret directive ordering the invasion of Poland no later than 1 September. The invasion plan was the work of Colonel Günther Blumentritt and generals Rundstedt and Manstein, though Hitler claimed it as his own.

On 23 May Hitler convened a meeting of the German General Staff, telling them of his determination 'to attack Poland at the first opportunity'. Lieutenant-Colonel Rudolf Schmundt noted: 'We cannot expect a repetition of the Czech affair. There will be war... The Führer doubts the possibility of a peaceful settlement with England... If we succeed in occupying and securing Holland and Belgium, as well as defeating France, the basis for a successful war against England has been created... There are no further successes to be achieved without bloodshed.'

Britain and France had failed to come to the aid of democratic Czechoslovakia, but now declared themselves ready to support a military junta. Hitler promised a stew they would choke on

Eve of War

Hitler believed that the ensuing war would be limited and over swiftly. There would be no world war as Britain was too decadent, France too degenerate and America too uninterested. None would sacrifice their sons for Poland.

On 21 August, Hitler put into place the last piece of the jigsaw. A non-aggression pact was signed between Nazi Germany and the Soviet Union. It contained a secret protocol. Following Hitler's invasion, the Soviet Union would take half of Poland, along with the Baltic states – Estonia, Latvia and Lithuania.

The Russians had another reason for siding with Hitler. They were simply not ready for war. Stalin's purges of the officer corps had decimated the Red Army leadership while the troops were equipped with obsolete weapons. All Hitler needed now was a pretext to invade.

November 1939: the serried ranks of Hitler's elite guard march with irresistible force through Prague as the occupying Germans enforce martial law following the execution of three Czech rebels

Chapter 2

WAR IN EUROPE

An armoured column of the Third Reich streams into Poland, igniting the war in Europe

The first shots of World War II were fired by men who were already dead. On 31 August 1939, the SS picked out a dozen male inmates from a concentration camp close to the Polish border and ordered them to dress in Polish army uniforms, before shooting them dead. The SS then staged a fake attack on the German radio station at Gliewitz on the Polish border.

They broadcast a brief message announcing the Polish invasion of Germany and dumped the bodies, making it look like they had been killed during an attack. The raid was code-named Operation Himmler. Now the Nazis were free to retaliate.

At dawn on 1 September 1939, a huge German army rolled across the 1,250-mile (2,000-km) Polish border. Immediately, Britain and France ordered a general mobilization. Their ambassadors in Berlin delivered identical messages to the German Foreign Ministry saying that, if Germany did not withdraw its troops from Poland, Britain and France would 'fulfil their obligations to Poland without hesitation'.

Britain had given Germany a deadline for its withdrawal from Poland – 0900 hours on 3 September. Two hours later, British Prime Minister Neville Chamberlain declared war. At midday, the French ambassador in Berlin called the German Foreign Minister Joachim von Ribbentrop, who told him that Germany refused to halt its invasion of Poland. France declared war at 1700 hours.

The fifty-five German armoured and motorized divisions that rolled over the Polish border on 1 September faced just seventeen infantry divisions, three infantry brigades and six cavalry brigades. Poland had mobilized only on 31 August, but thirteen divisions were still moving to their concentration areas, with another nine mustering in their barracks. While the Germans had modern arms and equipment, a large part of the Polish weaponry dated from the 1920s, and fast-moving German Panzers were faced by cavalry wielding lances. Against the Polish air force's 842 obsolescent planes, the Luftwaffe could put 4,700 modern aircraft in the air. German planes devastated Polish roads, railways, bridges and power stations, and terror-bombed the cities.

There was little Britain and France could do to help Poland. The French army had been prepared for defence not attack, and there were no British forces on the Continent until the first part of the British Expeditionary Force (BEF) took its place in the line at Lille, in France, on 3 October.

Nevertheless, the French did attack Germany on 7 September in Operation Saar. It was a disaster. To avoid violating Belgian neutrality, the French had to attack along the frontier between the Rhine and the Moselle, which had been drawn up after the defeat of Napoleon at Waterloo with the specific aim of discouraging French aggression. The Germans held the high ground and salients into French territory. The Germans had booby-trapped houses and laid cleverly sited fields of anti-tank and anti-personnel mines. The French

Victims of Nazi air strikes on Poland, September 1939 – many civilians were victims of the German dive-bombers

did not have any mine detectors. Beyond the border was the Siegfried Line, a German defensive wall built during the 1930s. To attack it, the French had to bring their artillery within range of the German batteries, which were well defended inside concrete casemates. French 155mm shells made little impression, and the heavier 220mm and 280mm shells were not fitted with delayed-action fuses which would have allowed them to penetrate the casemates before exploding. Although French fire was rapid and accurate, many of their shells, which were of World War I vintage, failed to explode.

In Poland, however, the Germans were demonstrating the effectiveness of their new tactic of Blitzkrieg. Armoured columns would race across the flat Polish landscape, with any defensive action being annihilated by dive-bombers. By 8 September, a German armoured corps was on the outskirts of the Polish capital, Warsaw, having advanced 140 miles (225 km) in seven days. The attack had been so swift that, by 10 September, Polish defence had been reduced to pockets of isolated troops.

By 13 September, the French decided that the Battle of Poland had been lost and the French advance into the Saarland, which was making no significant progress, was told to halt.

On 17 September, Soviet forces entered Poland

from the east. The following morning, the Polish government and high command crossed the Romanian frontier into exile, and formal resistance was over. The Warsaw garrison held out against the Germans until 28 September, while terror-bombings and artillery barrages reduced parts of the city to rubble with no regard for the civilian population. The last serious body of the Polish army held out until 5 October, although some guerrilla fighting went on into the winter. By then, Poland, as an independent state, had ceased to exist.

The swastika flies triumphantly over Westerplatte, Poland, September 1939

On 27 September 1939, Hitler told his generals that an offensive should be launched immediately against France to erase the humiliation of Germany's defeat in World War I. But first Hitler proposed a peace agreement on the basis of the partition of Poland. Britain and France declined. The Allies then watched the German build-up on the borders of Holland and Belgium with growing disquiet. However, heavy rain that autumn meant that Hitler had to postpone the attack no fewer than thirteen times. Due to the lack of activity, this period became known as the 'Phoney War'.

Following the invasion of Poland, Jews were compelled to wear a yellow star of David to identify them and, in the lands that the Germans had come to occupy, they were forced into ghettos.

The Race for Norway

Winston Churchill, then First Lord of the Admiralty, planned to lay mines in Norwegian waters to stop the export of Swedish iron ore to Germany. The British Cabinet also authorized Churchill to prepare a landing at the Norwegian port of Narvik.

Hitler feared that, if the British took Norway, they would blockade German ports and threaten Germany itself through the Baltic. On 9 April 1940, with the connivance of the leader of the Norwegian Fascist Party, Vidkun Quisling, Hitler invaded Norway, deploying paratroopers for the first time in warfare. Quisling was rewarded by becoming 'minister president' under a German commissioner. That same day, the German army – the Wehrmacht – overran Denmark, while Sweden managed to maintain its neutral status.

The British and French responded by sending in troops of their own to Norway and on 27 May took Narvik after fierce German resistance.

But then, the attack on France had begun and, only days after taking Narvik, the 25,000 Allied troops there were evacuated, leaving Norway in German hands.

Although the French were ill-equipped to attack, it had been thought that they were more than ready to defend themselves. In 1939, France had a standing army of 800,000 men, the largest in Europe at the time. Forty-one divisions manned the Maginot Line, thought to be impregnable. And while there were no fortifications along the Belgian border, it was defended by a further thirty-nine divisions.

The Dutch army had a conscript army of more than 400,000 men, but the Netherlands had managed to stay out of World War I, so these men had no experience of modern warfare. On 10 May, the Germans attacked with just seven divisions. Again they used paratroopers, who captured vital bridges at Rotterdam, Moerdij, and Dordrecht, while the German 9th Panzer Division raced across the country to link up with its airborne troops. On 11 May, the Dutch defenders fell back to Breda, along with the French Seventh Army, which had sped 140 miles (225 km) across Belgium to assist them. By midday on 12 May, German tanks were in the suburbs of Rotterdam. The Dutch retreated into the 'Fortress of Holland', the area north of the Maas and Waal rivers, to protect Amsterdam and

French soldiers push an ammunition cart through a tunnel deep inside the heart of the Maginot Line

Utrecht. But with few planes and few anti-aircraft guns, the Dutch had no defence against German air attacks. Queen Wilhelmina and her government escaped to England on 13 May, where she was later joined by the Norwegian king Haakon VII and his government. The Germans threatened to bomb Rotterdam and Utrecht if Dutch resistance continued and, on 14 May, the Netherlands capitulated – although the city of Rotterdam was bombed anyway due to a mix-up in German communications.

However, the main attack on France was to come through Belgium. On 10 May, German paratroops landed in gliders on the top of the fortress of Eben Emael, destroyed it with demolition charges and took key bridges. Although the invaders had only four army corps and one armoured corps, along with five hundred airborne troops, air attacks and terror-bombing quickly took their toll.

While the military situation deteriorated, on the evening of 10 May, Chamberlain resigned and was succeeded by Winston Churchill, who formed a national government.

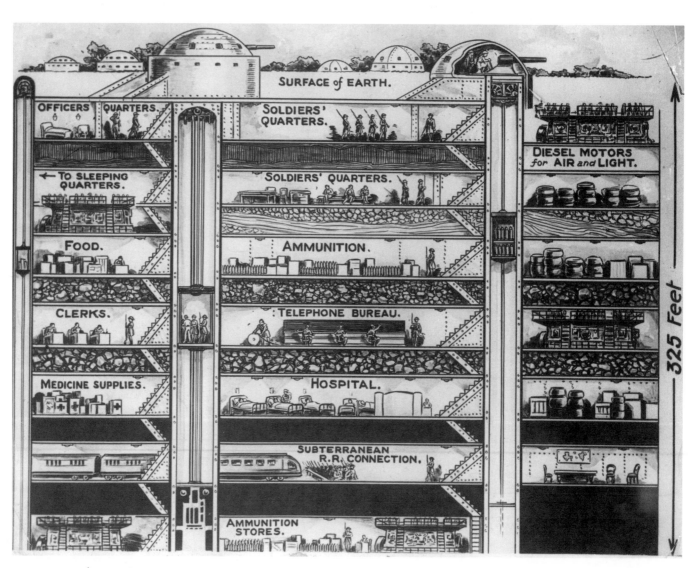

Cross-section of gun emplacements, Maginot Line

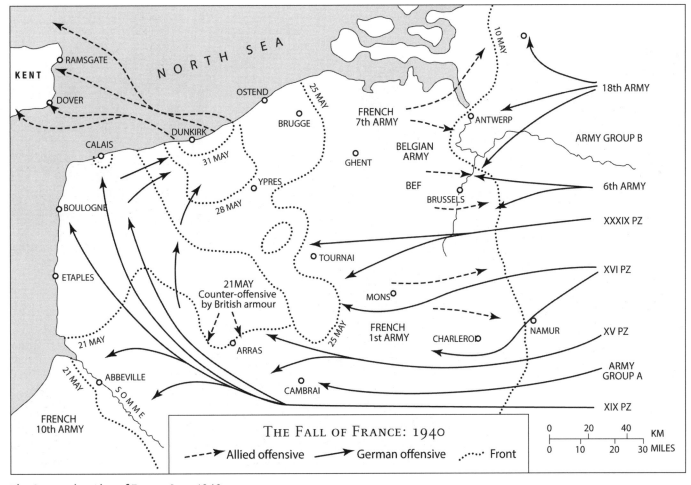

The German invasion of France, June 1940

The following day, the Belgian line collapsed, and German tanks swept through to take Liège from the rear. The Belgian army retreated to a defensive line along the river Dyle, where it was joined by British and French troops. Two tank divisions staged a set-piece battle to check the German advance. By 15 May, the Dyle Line had been outflanked and had to be abandoned.

Instead of the main attack coming through the perfect tank country between Liège and Namur, as it had in World War I, the thrust came on a narrow front through the Ardennes Forest, which the French thought could not be used by tanks due to the problems of keeping the units supplied over the tortuous mountain roads.

Again on 10 May, Field Marshal Gerd von Rundstedt threw 1,500,000 men and more than 1,500 tanks – two-thirds of Germany's forces in the west and nearly three-quarters of its tanks – against the weakest part of the front, which was defended by just twelve infantry divisions and four cavalry divisions mounted on horses. A thrust through Luxembourg took just three hours to cover the 30 miles (50 km) to the Belgian border. Another armoured thrust through the forest itself reached France in less than three days. The infantry followed. Not expecting an advance in this area, the French there had few anti-aircraft or anti-tank guns to take on

A destroyed bridge bars the way of German tanks, Belgium, 1940

the German dive-bombers or armoured columns; the French cavalry divisions which rode in on horseback to reinforce the sector were forced to retreat to the river Semois on 11 May.

The Road to Dunkirk

On 13 May, after the French defenders on the south bank had been devastated by waves of dive-bombers, German infantry crossed the Meuse on rafts and in rubber dinghies at Sedan – the site of France's defeat in the Franco-Prussian War of 1870. The French had just a handful of aircraft aloft, while the German thrust was supported by a thousand. The next day, German tanks crossed

the river and, on 15 May, they broke through what remained of the French defences. It was estimated that the Germans could be in Paris in two days. Instead, the Germans turned westwards towards the Channel. The following day, the German spearhead covered almost 50 miles (80 km) of open country. When the spearhead was joined by a diversionary force coming through Liège, French resistance collapsed.

The French and British had imagined that the German advance would sweep across Belgium to the coast and turn southwards, as it had in World War I. Instead, it swept southwards into France, then turned in an arc to the north in a move was known as the *Sichelschnitt* or 'sickle stroke'. It broke all communication between Allied forces north and south of this 'Panzer corridor', and the French and British forces that had advanced into Belgium were now threatened with encirclement.

As early as 19 May, the British commander Viscount Gort had considered withdrawing the BEF by sea, but the British government had not yet accepted that defeat was inevitable. So on 21 May, he launched an attack southwards from Arras against the Germans' right flank in an attempt to break through to the French forces to the south.

By that time, the head of the German column had swept through Boulogne and Calais. Dunkirk was now the only Channel port left through which the BEF could withdraw. The Allies had set up their final defence line along the Canal d'Aire outside Dunkirk. On 24 May, the Germans were crossing the canal, ready to make their final push to take the town, when Hitler ordered a halt to their advance.

The German dive-bombers had virtually had the skies to themselves up to this point, but as they approached the coast they found themselves under attack from Royal Air Force fighters based in England. Nevertheless, Göring promised Hitler that he could finish off the Dunkirk bridgehead with his Luftwaffe alone.

As it was, Gort did not have the armour to break through the Panzer corridor. Running short of supplies and ammunition, on 25 May, he ordered the BEF to fall back on Dunkirk. The British government now decided that it had to save what could be saved. Admiral Bertram Ramsay had been preparing for an evacuation from Dunkirk since 19 May. Already the call had gone out for small boats. Operation Dynamo, as the evacuation was called, began on 26 May. With the British in Belgium withdrawing towards Dunkirk, the Belgian army was left to face the Germans alone. On 27 May, it broke. The following day, King Leopold surrendered. Rather than go into exile, he remained under house arrest in Brussels for the rest of the war.

With Gort no longer a threat, Hitler ordered that the advance on Dunkirk be resumed. But the hiatus had allowed the British to consolidate their defences. When the order came to advance again, the Germans met considerable resistance. Almost immediately Hitler ordered the German armour to stop, thinking it best

British troops lie on their backs to shoot at German aircraft as the British Expeditionary Force is evacuated from the beach at Dunkirk, June 1940

to reserve the Panzers for use against the remaining French army under General Maxime Weygand to the south.

Amateur Sailors

The Luftwaffe began bombing the harbour at Dunkirk, putting it out of action. But the harbour's bomb-damaged breakwater was still serviceable and allowed many of the troops to be taken off by larger transports. The rest were picked up directly from a 10-mile (16-km) stretch of beach, where they mustered, by small craft largely manned by amateur sailors. In all, 848 British, French and Belgian ships of all shapes and sizes – from destroyers to private motor cruisers – joined the operation. In eight days, some 340,000 men, two-thirds of them British, were rescued, though almost all their equipment had been abandoned.

Another 220,000 Allied troops were rescued from Cherbourg, Saint-Malo, Brest, and Saint-

German Dornier 217 bombers fly over the Silvertown area of London's docklands during the Blitz, 1940. The old greyhound track at West Ham can be seen near the centre of the picture

Nazaire. But in three weeks the German army had taken more than a million men prisoner.

Although the BEF was now safely back in Britain, the Battle of France was not over. General Weygand could still muster forty-nine divisions, along with another seventeen still holding the Maginot Line. But the Germans had 140 divisions at their disposal, including ten divisions of tanks. On 5 June, the Wehrmacht started pushing southwards from the Somme. The French held the Germans for two days, but on 7 June Panzers under Major General Erwin Rommel broke through to the south-west. Two days later, they crossed the Seine. That same day, 9 June, the Germans broke through to the south-east, then made a dash for the Swiss border, cutting off the French forces still holding the Maginot Line, and the Battle of France was lost.

On 22 May 1940, Mussolini had signed a military alliance with Hitler, known as the 'Pact of Steel'. Then on 10 June, Mussolini declared war on France and Britain, and some thirty Italian divisions crossed the French frontier on 20 June.

As the Germans advanced, the French government under Paul Reynaud left Paris, fleeing south. On 14 June, the Germans entered Paris. Reynaud's position was now untenable and he resigned on 16 June. He was replaced by his deputy, the elderly Marshal Philippe Pétain, who was France's most-honoured soldier in World War I. That same day, General Charles de Gaulle, undersecretary for defence in Reynaud's administration, arrived in London. That night, Pétain's government requested an armistice. While the two sides discussed terms, the German advance continued until it had swallowed two-thirds of the country.

On 22 June 1940, the representatives of Germany and France met at Compiègne where the

German troops in front of the Arc de Triomphe. The speed of the Nazi victory in France took everyone, including Hitler, by surprise

armistice ending the war in 1918 had been signed in a railway carriage. Hitler came to Compiègne to watch the new armistice being signed in that same carriage. The carriage was then taken to Germany, where it was destroyed in April 1945 to prevent it falling into Allied hands.

The 1940 armistice divided France into two zones. Northern France, from the Swiss border to the English Channel and a western strip down the Atlantic coast to the Spanish border, was to be held under German military occupation. The rump of the country and its overseas possessions were to be left in the hands of a collaborationist government under Pétain, based at Vichy. However, on 18 June, de Gaulle began broadcasting appeals for France to continue the war from London, where he organized the Free French Forces.

Although the Battle of France had been decisively lost, there was one last action. Britain – with its Empire – now stood alone. Sea power was all-important, and the British government decided that it could not risk the French navy, which was technically under the control of Vichy, falling into German hands. Britain seized all French ships in ports under its control, but the French still possessed a considerable fleet at their naval base at Mers-el-Kébir in Algeria, then a French colony. On 3 July 1940, British ships appeared off the Algerian coast. When the French fleet refused to join the Allies or steam to a neutral port, the British opened fire, putting the fleet out of action and killing 1,297 French seamen.

The Battle of Britain

On 18 June 1940, Winston Churchill told a hushed House of Commons: 'What General Weygand called the "Battle of France" is over. I expect the "Battle of Britain" to begin.' However, having taken his revenge on France, Hitler once again sought to make peace, saying he would keep the Continent for himself while leaving Britain its overseas Empire. But as Britain showed no willingness to come to terms, Hitler began to prepare for battle once again.

The enemy, he knew, was in no position to resist him. In Great Britain and Northern Ireland, there were just twenty-nine divisions – including two Canadian divisions – and eight independent brigades, six of which were armoured. They were outnumbered four to one. What is more, the British were poorly equipped. On 8 June, they had just seventy-two tanks. This number was to increase to two hundred by August and 438 by September, but these tanks were already obsolescent.

In June 1940, the British Home Forces had just 420 field guns and 163 heavy guns, with 200 and 150 rounds each, respectively. The British two-pounder (40mm) guns – of which they had just fifty-four – were of little use against tanks. What was needed was 75mm guns, which had proved their

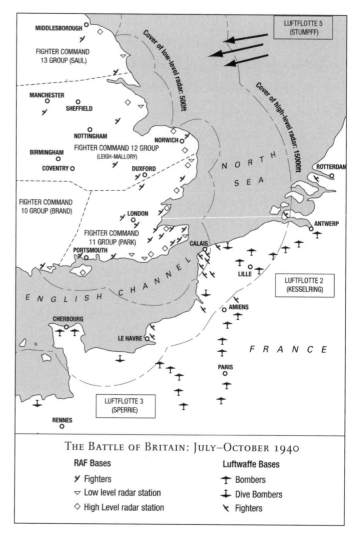

THE BATTLE OF BRITAIN: JULY–OCTOBER 1940

RAF Bases	Luftwaffe Bases
⌇ Fighters	⊥ Bombers
▽ Low level radar station	⊥ Dive Bombers
◇ High Level radar station	⋏ Fighters

The distribution of British and German airpower during the Battle of Britain

worth as tank-killers in the Battle of France. Fortunately, the United States allowed the British to take over arms contracts that the French had signed. Orders included 900 75mm guns with a thousand shells each, along with 500,000 rifles. The British had to pay cash for these and transport them to Britain themselves. The British Merchant Navy did this without suffering a single loss to U-boats.

For nearly a month after the fall of France, Hitler dallied, hoping that the British would settle. Then, on 16 July 1940, he signed Führer Directive

No. 16, which authorized Operation Sealion – the invasion of England. The month had not been wasted by the British. They had stepped up armament production and prepared their defences.

Operation Sealion was set to begin on 25 August. The invasion force would consist of forty-one divisions, six armoured and three motorized, along with two divisions of airborne troops. The Sixteenth Army would land between Ramsgate and Hastings, while the Ninth would land between Brighton and Littlehampton, with a detachment taking the Isle of Wight. This force under Field Marshal Gerd von Rundstedt would head for a line running from Gravesend through Reigate to Portsmouth. Soon after, the Sixth Army, which was mustered on the Cherbourg Peninsula, would land on the Dorset coast between Weymouth and Lyme Regis. It would strike towards Bristol, with a detachment taking Devon. At that same moment, the Ninth Army would break through the British defences on the North Downs, cross the Thames at Reading and encircle London from the west.

There was a problem, though. The commander of the Kriegsmarine (German navy) Grand Admiral Erich Raeder pointed out that, even if he were to requisition every available vessel from the fishing fleets and inland waterways – which would have devastating effects on food supplies and war production – he could not land the first wave of thirteen divisions, even if their numbers were hugely reduced. Besides, the Royal Navy was still a considerable fighting force, and Raeder did not think he would be able to give the invasion fleet sufficient protection. So the attack on Devon was dropped from the plan and the planned invasion force reduced to twenty-seven divisions.

A flight of Spitfires scrambled over the coast of England during the Battle of Britain

RAF Hurricane pilots scramble for their aircraft. Of the nearly 3,000 aircrew who fought, one in three were killed or wounded

The Germans did not have a battle fleet large enough to give the troops landing on the English beaches the necessary artillery support, and the Luftwaffe would not be able to provide total coverage either. So huge batteries were built along the French coast from Sangatte to Boulogne which would pound the invasion beaches. To provide the assault force with support when they got ashore, the Germans developed submarine tanks. These were regular Panzers that had been waterproofed and fitted with a flexible snorkel to feed air to the engine and the occupants. They would be dropped offshore by special landing craft, sink to the bottom in 25–30 feet (7.5–9 m) of water, then drive up onto the beaches. Experiments off the island of Sylt in the North Sea showed that the submarine Panzers worked perfectly. Even so, the German land forces would need the support of dive-bombers and, as a preliminary, massive Stuka attacks would be needed to destroy the British coastal defences. To do that, the Germans would need air superiority.

On 1 August 1940, Hitler signed Führer Directive No. 17, ordering the Luftwaffe to smash the RAF as quickly as it could. It was to take the RAF on in the air and attack its ground facilities and supply centres. It was to bomb aircraft factories and factories producing anti-aircraft guns. It was also to attack the ports which brought in vital supplies – though leaving intact the Channel ports which would be needed in the invasion. British cities, though, were not to be terror-bombed without the express order of Hitler himself.

The Germans deployed three air fleets against Britain. They flew from Norway and Denmark, Belgium and the Netherlands, and Northern France. Between them they had 2,442 aircraft – 969 heavy bombers, 336 dive-bombers, 869 single-engined fighters and 268 twin-engined fighters.

Although the RAF fighter force – some 620 aircraft – was considerably smaller than the Germans' 1,137, the British had not been sitting on their hands. Fighter production had risen from 157 a month in January 1940 to 496 in July. The RAF did, however, have a shortage of trained pilots.

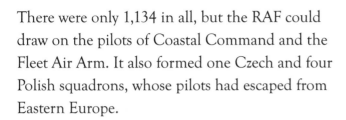

There were only 1,134 in all, but the RAF could draw on the pilots of Coastal Command and the Fleet Air Arm. It also formed one Czech and four Polish squadrons, whose pilots had escaped from Eastern Europe.

Wings of Death

The RAF's Hurricanes and Spitfires were much faster and more manoeuvrable than Germany's twin-engined Messerschmitt Bf 110 'destroyer' – which was also known as 'Göring's folly'. On the other hand, the single-seater Messerschmitt Bf 109E was faster than the Mark I Hurricane and about as fast as the Mark I and II Spitfires that were just appearing in frontline squadrons. The Bf 109 could also climb faster than the British fighters, but the British planes were more manoeuvrable. With eight machine guns, they could outshoot their German adversaries, and it is generally reckoned that the Spitfire, although in short supply, was unrivalled as an interceptor at that time.

German heavy bombers were vulnerable to attack from both Hurricanes and Spitfires, particularly in daylight, and did not have the bomb-carrying capacity to deliver a knockout blow. British fighters also found that German dive-bombers could be shot down easily, and German fighters could give them only partial protection, as they were fighting at the limit of their flying range.

The British had other advantages. Since 1938, the British had the most advanced radar defence network in the world, which stretched from Land's End in the south north to the Shetland Islands. Incoming German planes could be detected in time for commanders to get their fighters airborne, so they were not caught and destroyed on the ground. With this radar information, control centres could direct the fighters by radio to intercept the enemy, often taking the Germans by surprise.

As the battle was fought over home soil, the British were able to recover their downed pilots, whereas if a German aircraft was shot down both the plane and crew were lost.

> *As the battle was fought over home soil, the British were able to recover their downed pilots, whereas if a German aircraft was shot down both the plane and crew were lost*

Although there had been preliminary attacks in June and July, the air war began in earnest on 8 August with the Germans sending up to 1,500 aircraft a day to bomb the British airfields and radar stations. In fighting, on 8, 11, 12, and 13 August, the RAF lost eighty-eight planes, while the Luftwaffe lost 145 aircraft. Between 13 and 17 August, the RAF lost 184, against the Luftwaffe's 255. The battle was becoming so expensive that Göring withdrew *Luftflotte V* flying from Norway and Denmark, along with his Stuka dive-bombers. In late August, however, the Luftwaffe was close to winning the battle.

Essential British airfields were pitted with bomb craters. The RAF's effectiveness was further curtailed by bomb damage to its radar stations and operations centres which were sited on airfields. Aircraft were being destroyed on the ground, and it was becoming difficult to co-ordinate formations in the air.

Aircraft losses began to turn in Germany's favour. Between 24 August and 6 September, the

Luftwaffe lost 378 planes, against the RAF's 262. Although this appears to give the British an advantage of 45 per cent, the German losses included both bombers and fighters. The British were losing all-important fighters and their experienced pilots. Fighter Command had fewer than a thousand pilots. All of them were in action several times a day and desperately in need of rest. With fifteen to twenty pilots killed or wounded every day, Fighter Command was reaching its last gasp.

Salvation came by glorious accident. Late in the evening of 24 August, a German plane accidentally bombed non-military targets in London. Churchill immediately ordered a retaliatory attack on Berlin. The next night, eighty-one twin-engined bombers took off for the German capital. Only twenty-nine planes made it. The others became lost on the way. Eight men were killed and twenty-eight wounded. The damage to Berlin was slight, but Hitler had promised the German people that such a thing would never happen. Infuriated, he abandoned the 1 August Directive and ordered the terror-bombing of London. Britain's capital was about to receive the same treatment as Warsaw and Rotterdam.

The sustained German bombing campaign that followed became known as the Blitz – 'lightning'. It began on 7 September, when 330 tonnes of bombs were dropped on London. The terror-bombing campaign was later extended to Liverpool, Coventry and other cities. Although the population suffered terribly from these attacks, the switch of the Luftwaffe's objective gave Fighter Command the breathing space to recover. Between 7 and 30 September, the RAF downed 380 German aircraft for the loss of 178 of its own.

The German air offensive reached a peak on Sunday 15 September with a series of attacks during which British air defences claimed to have downed 185 German planes. The figure was later dropped to fifty-six. But it hardly mattered. The British had defeated the Germans in the air and were shooting down bombers faster than German factories could produce them. By 31 October, the Germans had lost 1,733 planes against Britain's 1,379, and Fighter Command had lost 414 men. So Churchill was not exaggerating when he told the House of Commons on 20 August 1940, 'Never in the field of human conflict has so much been owed by so many to so few.'

Even so, Hitler continued his preparations for Operation Sealion. While the troops of the Ninth and Sixteenth Armies gathered at their embarkation points, an invasion fleet comprising 2,500 transports, tugs, lighters, barges and fishing boats was assembled in ports from Le Havre to Rotterdam. The fleet then came under attack from the RAF's Bomber Command.

On 11 September, Hitler announced his intention of beginning the countdown to Sealion on 14 September – and the landings would begin at dawn on 24 September. But on 14 September, he postponed the decision for another three days, though 27 September was the last day the tides were favourable. And the strong winds and high seas that could be expected in the English Channel from October onwards would make an invasion impossible.

On 17 September, Hitler ordered that Sealion be postponed and, on 19 September, the invasion fleet was dispersed to protect it from further bombing. Hitler ordered that it should be dispersed in such a way that it could be rapidly reassembled.

Although daylight raids on British cities continued until the end of the month, German losses continued at such a rate

Paratroopers drop in during the German invasion of Crete. Despite the success of their mission, losses among airborne troops were so high that Hitler vowed never again to mount a similar operation

that, at the beginning of October, the Luftwaffe turned to night bombing. By the end of the month it was recognized that the Battle of Britain was over.

During the following months, the Luftwaffe continued its Blitz with night-time bombing raids on Britain's biggest cities. By February 1941, the bombing offensive had eased, but in March and April it was stepped up again. Some 10,000 sorties were flown, with the bombing concentrated on the East End of London. However, the Luftwaffe never turned its attention back to British airfields. By the time suitable weather for an invasion came the following spring, Hitler had turned his eyes eastwards.

The Invasion of Crete

In preparation for his attack on the Soviet Union, Hitler began drawing other central European countries – Hungary, Romania, Slovakia, Bulgaria, Yugoslavia – into the Axis. Following Germany's huge gains in the west, Italy began to find itself very much the junior partner in the Pact of Steel. Mussolini wanted to make some territorial gains of his own. Without informing Hitler, he sent 155,000 men across the border from Albania, which Italy had invaded in 1939, into Greece.

The British rallied to the defence of Greece, sending men and planes to air bases on the mainland near Athens. This put them within striking distance of the Romanian oilfields at Ploiesti which were vital for Germany's attack on Russia. Hitler had no option but to help Mussolini out. In March, there was a coup d'état against the pro-Axis regime in Belgrade, so the Germans decided to invade Yugoslavia with Italian support, and sweep through into Greece. They made a lightning thrust through the Balkans, forcing the British to evacuate. By 11 May, the whole of Greece and the Aegean islands, with the exception of Crete, were in German hands.

The British wanted to hold on to Crete. It was just 500 miles (800 km) from Alexandria and 200 miles (320 km) from Tobruk. The bastion of British resistance in North Africa, Tobruk had to be supplied by sea and would be in great danger if the Germans had the airfields on Crete.

Costly Acquisition

On 25 April 1940, Hitler's Führer Directive No. 28 ordered the invasion of Crete. He made it be known that the island had to be in German hands by the end of May so that he could concentrate on the invasion of Russia, which was scheduled for June. His commanders complied, but at enormous cost and to little strategic advantage. Hitler did not use the island as a base for dominating the eastern Mediterranean despite the sacrifice of four thousand men and the loss of more than three hundred aircraft, resources that might have been put to more effective use in Russia.

The Allies had also lost four thousand men, with another twelve thousand captured. A further seventeen thousand had been evacuated under the noses of the Germans in an operation that cost the Royal Navy two destroyers and three cruisers. But for the Germans it was a hollow victory. The German paratroopers had suffered heavy losses and had only won because of their sheer weight of numbers. Their parachute divisions had proven ineffective against ground troops who were dug in and well prepared. Eight days' fighting on Crete had cost the Germans more than the entire Balkan campaign. Hitler declared himself 'most displeased'. After Crete, Hitler forbade any further large-scale use of paratroops, and plans to invade Cyprus and, later, Malta were abandoned.

Chapter 3

WAR IN THE DESERT

After the fall of France, Mussolini feared that Hitler would make peace with the British, thwarting his territorial ambitions in the Mediterranean. Italy already had one possession in North Africa – Libya, which it had invaded in 1911. So when the British rejected Hitler's overtures, Mussolini turned his attention to Egypt, which had been in British hands since 1882. He ordered Marshal Rodolfo Graziani to launch an offensive eastwards against the British troops in Egypt who were under the command of General Sir Archibald Wavell.

On 13 September 1940, the Italian Tenth Army took the small border port of Sollum. They then advanced a further 50 miles (80 km) into Egypt and occupied the British base at Sidi Barrani on 16 September. Six weeks later, the British Western Desert Force under Lieutenant General Richard O'Connor started a 'five-day raid' which pushed the Italians back across the border on 10 December. Reinforced by Australians, the Western Desert Force continued the advance and took the small port of Tobruk in north-east Libya on 21 January 1941. By the time the Italians surrendered on 7 February, the British had driven them back 500 miles (800 km), taking more than 130,000 prisoners, as well as 400 tanks and 1,290 guns. Meeting no further resistance, the Western Desert Force could have gone on to take Tripoli, but its supply lines were already overstretched and Churchill wanted to divert men and resources to Greece.

The Siege of Tobruk

Again Hitler came to Mussolini's aid. On 6 February, he sent General Erwin Rommel and his newly formed Afrika Korps to Tripoli. On 24 March, Rommel attacked at El Agheila, capturing O'Connor and pushing the British column back the way it had

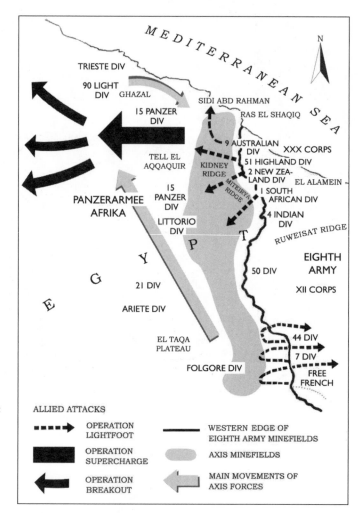

The Alamein battles October–November 1942

come. Wavell decided, however, to hold Tobruk while the rest of the British force retreated into Egypt to regroup. It was to be defended by the 9th Australian Division, reinforced by a brigade of the 7th and the Sikhs of the 18th Cavalry Regiment. Major General Leslie Morshead, commander of the 9th, told his men, 'There will be no Dunkirk here. If we have to get out, we will fight our way out. No surrender and no retreat.'

On 10 April, Rommel reached Tobruk and sent a motorized detachment to storm the town, but it was repulsed by heavy gunfire which killed its commander. Three nights later, the Germans were repulsed again.

Meanwhile, elements of the Afrika Korps had bypassed Tobruk and had reached the Egyptian border. From then on, the 22,000 men at Tobruk would have to be supplied by sea. However, while the Luftwaffe had complete air superiority, Allied anti-aircraft gunners managed to keep the harbour open.

Over the next two months, Panzers made repeated attacks that were fended off. By then the Germans had lost 1,700 men, compared to the garrisons' casualties of 797 – 59 killed, 355 wounded and 383 missing. However, the German High Command grew alarmed at the losses and ordered Rommel not to attack again. However, Nazi radio propagandist William Joyce – a US citizen hanged for treason after the war, and known in Britain as 'Lord Haw Haw' because of his sneering voice –

crowed that the garrison was 'caught like rats in a trap'. A German newspaper then dubbed the British defenders the 'Rats of Tobruk', a name they embraced, calling themselves 'Desert Rats'. Rommel now laid siege and repulsed three attempts for reinforcements to break through. Eventually the Axis forces were forced back and the garrison relieved.

The Siege of Tobruk lasted 242 days from 10 April to 7 December 1941, fifty-five days longer than the siege of Mafeking in the Boer War. It was the first defeat of German land forces in

Tourist shot: a British tank crew poses in front of a pyramid, Egypt 1941

Soldiers of the British 7th Armoured Division, the 'Desert Rats', pose with a field gun before the fall of Tobruk, 1942

World War II and showed that the Blitzkrieg could be defeated by minefields, artillery, anti-aircraft fire and infantry who stood their ground.

As well as providing a vital psychological boost, the defence of Tobruk also kept Turkey – Germany's ally in World War I – out of the war.

This prevented Hitler from using Turkey as a southern springboard for his attack on the Soviet Union and delayed it by at least a month. As winter is considered to be Russia's greatest general, this proved crucial.

The Drive on Gazala

Following the relief of Tobruk, Rommel was driven back to El Agheila, where the British advance had first halted in February 1941. With the attack on Pearl Harbor in December 1941 and Japan's rapid advance on Britain's colonies in the Far East, the Allies turned their attention there, starving the desert forces of supplies. During his retreat from Tobruk, however, Rommel had been supplied with new tanks. In January 1942, a convoy arrived in Tripoli carrying more reinforcements. Soon the

Afrika Korps had 111 tanks with twenty-eight more in reserve, while the Italians had eighty-nine.

Rommel quickly counterattacked, destroying nearly half of the British armour. In the swift reversal, the Desert Fox, as Rommel had now become known, captured huge quantities of supplies as, once again, he made a dash eastwards. By 6 February, he had pushed the British back to Gazala, just 30 miles (50 km) west of Tobruk. There the British retreated behind a mine field that ran 30 miles southwards from the coast where they hoped to build up their strength. The problem with any defensive line in the North African campaign was that it inevitably had an open flank at the desert end. Rommel simply drove round it.

After eighteen days' fierce fighting, the British were forced back to the Egyptian frontier. This time Tobruk fell. Winston Churchill was in Washington when he heard the news. It was a national disaster. Throughout 1941, the defiance of the small garrison at Tobruk of the might of the German army had been a beacon of hope. Now that beacon had been extinguished. Hitler, on the other hand, was delighted and promoted Rommel to the rank of field marshal. And with the stores he had captured at Tobruk, Rommel could push on into Egypt before the British had time to regroup.

El Alamein

The Allies thought that they could delay Rommel's advance with a line of fortification General Neil Ritchie, then commanding the Eighth Army, had built running south along the Egyptian border from Sollum to Sidi Omar. But this suffered from the same tactical weakness as the Gazala Line – the desert flank remained open. Rommel swept around it on 24 June, advancing more than 100 miles (160 km) in one day. However, realizing that the line could not be held, the Eighth Army had already fallen back to Mersa Matruh, 120 miles (200 km) east of the frontier. The situation was now desperate. The Luftwaffe was already in range of Alexandria. And if the Eighth Army failed to hold back Rommel, there was nothing to stop him taking Egypt, the Suez Canal and the oilfields of the Persian Gulf, then going on to attack the beleaguered Russians' southern flank.

Ritchie intended to make one final stand at Mersa Matruh, but Wavell's successor General Sir Claude Auchinleck realized that a defensive line there would suffer exactly the same weaknesses as those at Gazala and Sollum. On 25 June, he sacked Ritchie and took personal command of the Eighth Army. The next day he issued new orders. There would be no new line at Mersa Matruh. Instead, he intended to keep his all troop formations fluid. Mobile columns would strike at the enemy from all sides. To that end, he reorganized into brigade battle groups made up of artillery – always the Western Desert Force's strength – supported by armour and infantry.

On 27 June, the Axis caught up with the Allies again. There was a series of punishing skirmishes with units of the British forces being bypassed, cut off and having to break out eastwards. Eventually, they fell back on a line at El Alamein, just 60 miles (100 km) from Alexandria. There, Auchinleck blocked any further advance.

What was different about Auchinleck's line at El Alamein, compared with that at Gazala, 350 miles (560 km) to the west, was that the El Alamein line did not have an open flank to the south. It ended at the Qattara Depression, 7,000 square miles (18,130 sq. km) of salt lakes and marshes impassable to tanks

Montgomery gave the beleagured British the will to defeat Rommel, the 'Desert Fox'

and other heavy military vehicles. The German spearhead reached the El Alamein line on 30 June. It was manned by Australians who had been the original 'desert rats' of Tobruk, along with British, South African, New Zealand and Indian troops who had fallen back across the desert. And at El Alamein, critically, they would be supported by the RAF.

Having come so far, so fast, the Afrika Korps was now exhausted. And it was at the end of a very long supply line. Its first assaults failed to break through, so it halted to build up its forces, and began to lay minefields. Throughout July 1942, assault was met with counterstroke, with neither side giving way.

On 13 July, Rommel launched his newly re-equipped Afrika Korps into what became known as the First Battle of El Alamein. Again the Panzers were halted and, that night, Auchinleck counter-attacked. Indians and New Zealanders overwhelmed two Italian divisions, and held off a counterstrike by the Panzers.

The battle became a war of attrition, leaving some 10,000 dead. Rommel quickly used up all the supplies that he had taken at Tobruk. He had been reinforced with 260 tanks but, after the fall

of Tobruk, US President Frankin D. Roosevelt had sent the British a hundred self-propelled guns and three hundred Sherman tanks. The Shermans were armed with 75mm guns that at last gave the British a tank to rival the Mark III and Mark IV Panzers.

Although Auchinleck had stopped Rommel's advance, he had not thrown him back and, on 4 August, Churchill arrived in Cairo to see what could be done. Auchinleck told him that he intended to delay any offensive until September to give the new reinforcements that he had just received time to acclimatize. Churchill sacked him and appointed Sir Harold Alexander Commander in Chief in the Middle East. Command of the Eighth Army was given to General Bernard Montgomery, who took over on 13 August. Montgomery quickly reorganized the Eighth Army again so that it fought in divisions, with units giving each other mutual support.

The Eighth Army was expecting Rommel to go on the offensive at some time around the full moon on 26 August. It was anticipated that he would attack, as usual, to the south of the line, aiming to break through, surround the Eighth Army within a matter of hours and rush on to take Cairo. The spot Rommel would choose for his attack was defended only by a minefield. But Montgomery had spotted the weakness in his defences too. Behind it he prepared positions so that any attacking force would have to run the gauntlet between six-pounder anti-tank guns and dug-in tanks.

Rommel's long supply lines meant that he had problems obtaining fuel. This delayed the attack until 31 August, giving the Allies more time to prepare. He had been hoping that his attack would take the British by surprise. But two hours before the attacking force – two hundred Panzers, 243 Italian medium tanks and thirty-eight light tanks –

set off, it came under attack from the RAF. Troops advancing in front of the tanks to lift the British mines came under heavy fire from well dug-in troops. More air strikes were called in. The commander of the Afrika Korps was badly wounded; the commander of the 21st Panzer Division was killed.

Rommel narrowed the front. His column made its way through two minefields, but was stopped by a third. The Panzers also found that they could make only slow progress on the soft sand. Casualties were heavy, and the stalled column came under artillery fire. But then a sandstorm blew up, grounding the RAF and hampering the artillery.

> *The Panzers found they could make only slow progress on the soft sand. Casualties were heavy, and the stalled column came under artillery fire. But then a sandstorm blew up...*

On 1 September, the storm lifted and the Panzers continued their advance. British armour drove them back. They tried another offensive in the afternoon, but were beaten back again. Montgomery tightened a ring of steel around the Afrika Korps. It tried to break out and failed, sustaining heavy casualties. Meanwhile, it was being bombed day and night. By the afternoon of 3 September, Rommel's men were in retreat. Montgomery now aimed to go on the offensive, but he did not feel that his reinforcements were sufficiently welded together to give chase. As it was, he let the Germans hold on to a strongpoint between the two minefields at the end of the El Alamein line.

New Preparations

On 7 September, Montgomery broke off the battle and began making new preparations. He had worked out a plan of deception to keep the enemy's strength at the south end of the line. He deployed a dummy pipeline, dummy supply dumps and dummy vehicles in that sector. Radio traffic was stepped up in the southern part of the line to suggest that an attack would be launched from there early in November.

The real attack, though, would be launched further north. The guns and tanks massed there were moved in at night and camouflaged carefully. Slit trenches were dug out into the desert for the infantry to attack from. These, too, were camouflaged to prevent German aerial reconnaissance knowing the British intentions. As the six-week period of preparation grew to a close, the RAF stepped up its attacks on enemy airfields, effectively grounding the Luftwaffe by 23 October – the night of the attack.

Montgomery abandoned the conventional wisdom of desert warfare. He would not attack to the south and try to turn the flank. Nor would he take on the enemy's armour, then deal with the infantry later. He would begin by sending a diversionary force against the armour in the south to make Rommel think that the main thrust would come there. Meanwhile,

British cavalry charge in North Africa [date uncertain]. Actions of this sort were rare on any front in World War II: most 'cavalry' units were in fact by this time equipped with tanks

there would be a massive bombardment, first of the artillery positions in the north, then the infantry positions there. Next, Montgomery's infantry would infiltrate down the slit trenches to take on German troops still dazed from the bombardment. While there would inevitably be vicious hand-to-hand fighting, Montgomery reckoned his men would get the best of it. The armour would then pour through the hole made by the infantry, systematically finish off the German infantry, and get into position at the rear to take on any remaining armour on ground of his choosing. Even if he could not destroy the Panzers completely, without infantry they could not hold ground and would have to retreat.

There was a full moon on the night of 23 October. This was vital, as thousands of mines would have to be lifted to make a hole in the enemy's defences. The minefields were 5,000–9,000 yards (4,570–8,230 m) in depth, and strengthened with booby-trap bombs and barbed wire. At 2140 hours, the Second Battle of El Alamein began, when more than 1,000 guns along the whole line opened fire simultaneously on the German artillery. Twenty minutes later, they switched their aim to the enemy's forward positions. As a huge curtain of dust and smoke rose over the enemy, the British infantry moved in with fixed bayonets to the skirl of the pipes.

The Germans resisted valiantly, but by 0530 the next morning two corridors had been opened, and the armour began moving down them. Then things began to go wrong. The infantry still had not made it all the way through the minefields when it was met with fierce resistance. This left the armour dangerously exposed. By dusk the following day, one column of armour had made it through. But the 10th Armoured Division was still in the middle of the minefields and taking shelter behind the

Miteiriya Ridge. Its commander General Herbert Lumsden had always been critical of Montgomery's plan. He thought that it was suicide to send tanks through narrow corridors in minefields where there was heavy anti-tank artillery, well dug in. If one tank was hit, those behind it could not move and would be sitting ducks.

In the Balance

Lumsden was summoned to Montgomery's HQ and explained his position. Montgomery then called Brigadier Alec Gatehouse who was commanding the spearhead, and ordered him to send the 10th Armoured Division over the ridge. Gatehouse refused to waste his division in such a reckless fashion. After a robust exchange of views, Montgomery ordered him to send one regiment over the ridge, instead of the entire division. Of the forty-nine tanks of the Staffordshire Yeomanry that went over, only fifteen limped back.

Nevertheless, the advance continued and, by the morning of 25 October, two armoured columns had reached the enemy's positions. But the situation on the battlefield had grown confused. The Germans made a number of bloody counterattacks. One, on the vital salient known as Kidney Ridge, was led by Rommel himself. All were repulsed. Gradually, things turned in Britain's favour. On 27 October, 1st Armoured Division alone knocked out fifty German tanks, and repeated sorties by the RAF broke up the Panzer formations.

With the two armies locked in fierce fighting, it became apparent to Rommel that everything depended on which side would be exhausted first. However, Montgomery had been skilfully pulling units out of the line to build up a force that could deliver a knockout punch. Those that remained

In his natural element: Rommel's tactical skills and resourcefulness were admired by Hitler

were told to adopt a defensive posture, but to use aggressive patrolling and artillery fire to give the impression that the advance was continuing.

On the night of 28 October, the 9th Australian Division drove a wedge down the coastal road. This was what Rommel was hoping for. If the British attempted to move around him to the north, he could cut their forces in two. Hence he moved his Panzers to the north. Montgomery, however, did not follow up with a major attack down the coast. Instead, he sent the 2nd New Zealand Division against a weak point in the German line which was defended by the Italians.

The battle was reaching its climax. Rommel told his commanders that they must fight to the death, although shortage of fuel meant that he was already considering withdrawing. Then, on the night of 30 October, he thought he had got lucky. The Australians came up out of their trenches and moved forward against fierce resistance. This would inevitably exhaust the tenacious Australians. But a force of Panzergrenadiers – elite infantry transported in trucks for speed of movement – found themselves surrounded in a fortified position known as 'Thompson's Post'. The Panzers attacked repeatedly in an attempt to relieve them. After three days of fighting, they managed to get through to the survivors.

Meanwhile, in Operation Supercharge, the full weight of Montgomery's remaining forces was thrown against a 4,000-yard (3,660-m) stretch of the front. At 0100 on 2 November, two British infantry brigades moved through the New Zealanders' lines and attacked. They were followed by 123 tanks of the 9th Armoured Brigade. The objective was to destroy the anti-tank screen, especially the lethal 88mm guns. Montgomery told its commander Brigadier John Currie, 'I am prepared to accept one hundred per cent casualties.' Currie led the attack personally.

Outmanoeuvred

The tanks, which were followed by infantry with bayonets fixed, ran over mines. As the sun came up, they were hit by dug-in German anti-tank guns. All but nineteen of the 9th Armoured Brigade's tanks were knocked out, and 230 of Currie's four hundred men were killed; however, the attack succeeded in its objective. Through the new corridor it had created plunged the 1st Armoured Division. When Rommel realized that he had been tricked, he sent formations of Panzers south. The following day anti-tank guns were moved into position, but by that time the British had expanded their salient to the south and were pushing relentlessly westwards. A tank battle ensued, but the German and Italian tanks were held in check by the RAF and artillery fire. After two hours, the German counterattack petered out. That afternoon, Rommel tried again, throwing an Italian armoured division into the fray. But more and more British reinforcements were pouring through the gap and fanning out behind it.

The Afrika Korps was down to just thirty-five tanks when Rommel decided to withdraw. But he received an order from Hitler, telling him to hold the position to the last man.

Turning Tail

Rommel knew that to hold his current position would be suicidal. But then, it would also be suicidal to disobey Hitler. When General von Thoma, head of the Afrika Korps, asked for permission to retreat, Rommel refused, but he turned a blind eye when Thoma pulled back anyway. Thoma was captured soon after and did not have to face Hitler's wrath. After twelve days of fighting, the Axis forces were now in full retreat. Fuel was low and there were only enough vehicles for the Germans to get away. The hapless Italians were abandoned, and surrendered by the thousand.

Brigadier Gatehouse wanted the 10th Armoured Division to give pursuit. He was sure that he could outrun them in 48 hours and destroy them. But Montgomery was more cautious. Rommel had already shown that he could suddenly mount a counter-attack that could turn a rout into a new offensive. The retreating column was bombed and strafed by the RAF, and the 8th Armoured Brigade managed to head off a German column taking a large number of prisoners, tanks and lorries. Other units also gave pursuit, but a downpour on 7 November turned the road into a quagmire, and the Afrika Korps got away. It left 10,000 men behind it. Another 20,000 Italians had been captured. A further 20,000 had been killed or wounded. On the battlefield, there were 450 knocked-out tanks, along with seventy-five abandoned by the Italians due to lack of fuel. More than a thousand enemy guns had been destroyed or abandoned.

During the Battle of Alamein, the British Eighth Army sustained 13,500 casualties. Some five hundred British tanks had been knocked out – though 350 of those could be repaired – and a hundred guns were lost. In Britain, the church bells had been silent for years as they were to act as an invasion alarm. Churchill ordered that they be rung out in celebration. Speaking of the victory at El Alamein at the Mansion House in the City of London on 10 November 1942, he said memorably, 'Now is not the end. It is not even the beginning of the end. But it is, perhaps, the end of the beginning.'

For Britain, the Battle of Alamein was a turning point. For three years, the British had been battered in Europe, on the Atlantic and in the Far East.

'Before Alamein we never had a victory,' wrote Churchill. 'After Alamein we never had a defeat.'

For Britain, the Battle of Alamein was a turning point. 'Before Alamein we never had a victory,' wrote Churchill. 'After Alamein we never had a defeat'

Operation Torch

The United States had joined the war after the Japanese attacked Pearl Harbor on 7 December 1941. On 11 December, Hitler had declared war on the United States, and the United States declared war on Germany and Italy. The strategy agreed between Britain and the United States was that they should take on Hitler before dealing with the Japanese. The United States would maintain only defensive operations in the Pacific, while the bulk of its effort would go into defeating the Axis powers. As soon as the United States joined the war, the US military had wanted to launch an amphibious assault on the coast of France. But after two years of

fighting, the British were more cautious and persuaded the United States to join in the fight in an area of the world where they had already had some success – North Africa.

On 8 November 1942, with Rommel in full retreat from El Alamein, a 117,000-strong Anglo-American task force under General Dwight D. Eisenhower was to land in French North Africa. Some 45,000 men under Major General George S. Patton would sail directly from the United States and seize Casablanca and the Atlantic coast of Morocco. Another 39,000 US troops under Major General Lloyd R. Fredendall would sail from Scotland and take the Mediterranean port of Oran in Algeria, while a 33,000-man Anglo-American force under Major General Charles Ryder would take the port of Algiers itself. The landings were to be code-named Operation Torch.

The situation in French North Africa was far from clear, and the landing forces met some resistance by French troops loyal to Vichy. Then when a cease-fire was called, the Germans claimed this was a violation of the armistice Pétain had signed, and invaded unoccupied France. What remained of the French Fleet then scuttled its ships in Toulon.

While General Patton's troops remained in Morocco training, the rest of the Allied forces turned east towards the western border of Tunisia – with Rommel's Afrika Korps retreating towards its eastern border. With Libya lost, Hitler was determined to hold on to the key ports of Tunis and Bizerte.

The British First Army, under Lieutenant General Kenneth Anderson, was to lead the assault on Tunis. Arriving at the Tunisian border, he found it strongly defended, and his first assault was repulsed. The major threat came from the Luftwaffe in Tunisia. The nearest Allied all-weather air base was at Bône,

120 miles (190 km) from the front lines. The Luftwaffe's nearest air base was just 5 miles (8 km) from the battlefield.

By the end of November 1942, the Axis forces in Tunisia had grown in size to around 25,000 men. They were supported by seventy Panzers – twenty of which were armed with the new 88mm guns. Nevertheless Field Marshal Albert Kesselring, Commander in Chief in the Mediterranean, sent a further three divisions.

In December, Anderson made a second attempt to take Tunis, but the Allied forces were inexperienced. Neither the British First Army nor the US II Corps had been tried in battle. However, a joint British–French–US force reached Longstop Hill overlooking the Gulf of Tunis in December. The battle there lasted four days, until a powerful German counter-attack supported by tanks brought the Allies to a halt. Any attempt to take Tunis would now have to be postponed. From the end of December to March, the rains come to North Africa, turning the parched landscape into a sea of mud.

Against the inexperienced Allies, Hitler sent Colonel General Hans-Jürgen von Arnim from the Eastern Front to take command of the Fifth Panzer Army and the defence of Tunisia. Arnim had more

Night firing: British 25-pounder field gun in action during the Battle of Gazala, June 1942

than 100,000 veteran German troops under his command and, by January 1943, he had all the mountain passes around Tunis under Axis control.

When Montgomery reached Tripoli in late January 1943, he stopped for rest and essential repair work. Rommel halted when he reached the Tunisian border and established the formidable Mareth Line there. He knew that he could not defeat Montgomery's veteran Eighth Army. But if he could hold them with minimal troops at the Mareth Line, he could launch an attack on the inexperienced and ill-supplied troops to his rear, then push along the Western Dorsal to the coast near Bône, knocking out the Allied airfield. However, Arnim favoured a more limited attack to strengthen his position on the Eastern Dorsal.

Heavy Casualties

On 14 February, German dive-bombers attacked the American forces guarding the town of Sidi Bou Zid in the Faid Pass. Then the tanks and infantry of the 10th Panzer quickly overran them, inflicting huge losses. The 21st Panzers attacked from the south through the Maizila Pass. By noon, the defenders of Sidi Bou Zid had been routed. The Americans quickly counter-attacked with a force of light tanks and infantry on half-tracks. The Americans lost more than 2,000 men, of which 1,400 were taken prisoner. Only 300 escaped. Some ninety-four tanks were lost, along with sixty half-tracks and twenty-six self-propelled guns. But Arnim would not give Rommel the support he needed to follow up on this success.

Rommel had won another tactical victory at the Kasserine Pass, but it was a strategic failure. Allied reinforcements were on their way. He had lengthened his supply lines, and his flanks were now open

to attack. And it would only be a matter of time before Montgomery turned up at the Mareth Line. Rommel called off the offensive on 22 February.

In early March, Rommel advanced again – this time towards Medenine and Montgomery's advancing forces. By this time Montgomery knew Rommel well and Rommel found himself attacking across open terrain against 810 medium, field and anti-tank guns, including many of the new 17-pounder anti-tank guns in use for the first time. Salvos of concentrated fire knocked out fifty-two tanks and inflicted 640 casualties before the Germans retreated. Again, Montgomery expressly forbade his men to pursue the fleeing enemy. Two days later, Rommel – now out of favour with Hitler – left Africa and his command was ceded to Arnim.

With the Germans now on the retreat in the west, General Harold Alexander, now in overall command, planned for his ground forces to tie up with the Eighth Army, which was massing to punch its way through the Mareth Line. The Eighteenth Army Group, as the combined command was known, would then bottle the Axis forces up in northern Tunisia, while the Allied air forces and navies would deny them escape or reinforcement.

Alexander insisted that hardened British troops should enter battle before inexperienced American ones. However General Patton had other ideas. When ordered to stage a diversionary attack to draw troops from the Mareth Line, Patton planned an offensive that would cut the Axis forces in two.

'Gentlemen, tomorrow we attack,' he told his commanders. 'If we are not victorious, let no one come back alive.'

Despite heavy rains, on the night of 16 March, Patton's 1st Infantry Division took the town of Gafsa. Arnim reacted as Alexander had predicted and sent the 10th Panzers to defend the passes that led from the Eastern Dorsal to the sea. The 10th Panzer arrived at the Maknassy Pass on 22 March, just as the 1st Armored Division also made it there. General Ward, commanding, realized that they had already exceeded Alexander's orders. He was also fearful of the Luftwaffe, which was flying from bases nearby, so he stopped to regroup. Patton was furious and sacked Ward.

The following day, an armoured battle group of the 10th Panzers advanced across an open plain. It was ambushed by tank destroyers, massed artillery and the 1st Infantry Division, which lay in wait in the hills. By the time they withdrew in disarray, the Germans had lost thirty-two tanks and large numbers of infantrymen.

By the standard of the war, the Battle of El Guettar was a small engagement, but to the Americans it was a decisive battle. They had shown the Germans – and the British, too – that they could fight. Naturally, Patton then wanted bigger fish to fry.

'Let me meet Rommel in a tank,' he said, 'and I'll shoot it out with the son-of-a-bitch.'

Unfortunately, Rommel was back in Germany and well out of Patton's reach by then.

While Patton was making his thrust down the Eastern Dorsal, Montgomery launched his offensive against the Mareth Line on 19 March. Using the same tactics as Rommel, he sent New Zealand Corps around the south end of the line, supported by the Desert Air Force. After nine days' fighting, the Axis forces fell back, before turning to fight again. After another furious battle which cost the British 1,300 casualties, the remains of the German and Italian forces fell back to Endifaville, just 50 miles (80 km) short of Tunis.

The Battle for Tunis

The American 34th Division was to take the pass at Fondouk in a frontal attack. The assault failed, with heavy casualties, and the 34th was withdrawn for retraining. This sparked another war of words between British and American commanders.

By then, the Axis forces were confined to a small enclave at the tip of the Tunisian peninsula, but it was clear that they would not give up without a fight. Alexander drew up Operation Strike to finish them off. Once again he gave the Americans only a minor role. However Eisenhower persuaded Alexander to change his plan and let the US II Corps take Bizerte.

Key to the success of the attack was a German strongpoint called Hill 609. The 34th Division was assigned to the task. The result was one of the most ferocious actions in the entire campaign.

The 1st Armored Division restored its tarnished glory with a thrust through the German defences on the road to Mateur, breaking the back of Bizerte's defences and cutting the Axis forces' only escape route. Arnim was determined to fight on, but Hitler turned a deaf ear to his requests for more ammunition and supplies. By then, the remains of the Axis forces were encircled on the plain of Tunis and, on 12 May, Arnim surrendered along with 250,000 crack troops – at a time when tens of thousands more were being wasted on the Eastern Front.

Overall Allied loses between 12 November 1942 and 13 May 1943 were 70,341. The French had lost 16,180; the British 35,940. The Americans had lost 18,221, including 2,715 killed. Tunisia, however, had been the American proving ground. General Omar Bradley said, 'In Africa we learned to crawl, to walk, to run.'

Chapter 4
THE RUSSIAN FRONT

Hitler was an avowed anti-Communist. Nevertheless, on 23 August 1939, his foreign minister Joachim von Ribbentrop and Soviet Commissar of Foreign Affairs Vyacheslav Molotov had signed the Nazi-Soviet Non-Aggression Pact, also known as the Molotov-Ribbentrop Pact. Then when they divided Poland between them that September Nazi-Soviet co-operation was said to be 'cemented in blood'.

But Hitler had no intention of honouring the Non-Aggression Pact. In February 1941, British intelligence learned that Germany planned to invade the Soviet Union that spring. The United States picked up similar information. Both informed Moscow. Stalin refused to believe it.

Then, seemingly out of the blue, the German ambassador in Moscow went to see Molotov and, at 0530 on 22 June 1941, he delivered a declaration of war. The reason – or excuse – was 'gross and repeated violations' of the Molotov-Ribbentrop Pact. A huge German army was already pouring across a 1,900-mile (3,000-km) front from the Baltic to the Black Sea. Even though the Soviets had been tipped off, the Germans achieved total surprise. Stalin had believed it when he had been told that the Axis forces massing on his borders were there for military manoeuvres.

In Operation Barbarossa, named for the 12th-century German founder of the First Reich, Hitler threw some 180 divisions into Russia – more than three million German troops, supported by thirty Romanian and Finnish divisions. There were nineteen Panzer divisions with 3,000 tanks; 2,500 aircraft were involved along with 7,000 artillery pieces. The German forces were divided into three army groups. The first, Army Group North, was commanded by Field Marshal Wilhelm von Leeb;

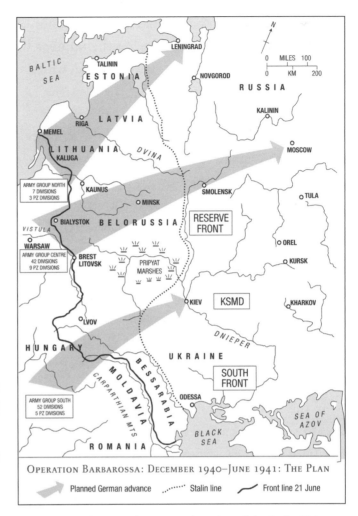

OPERATION BARBAROSSA: DECEMBER 1940–JUNE 1941: THE PLAN

→ Planned German advance   ······· Stalin line   ⌐ Front line 21 June

Operation Barbarossa, the German invasion of the Soviet Union, June 1941

the second, Army Group Centre, by Field Marshal Fedor von Bock; while the third, Army Group South, was commanded by Field Marshal Gerd von Rundstedt. The plan was to destroy all Soviet resistance in lightning advances on Leningrad (St Petersburg), Moscow and Kiev.

'We have only to kick in the door,' said Hitler to Rundstedt, 'and the whole rotten structure will come crashing down.'

It was said that Stalin had a 'nervous collapse' when he was told of the invasion. He did not speak for eleven days. The Soviet Union, however, was hardly defenceless in the face of this attack. Stalin had twice or maybe even three times the number of tanks and aircraft the Germans had and, while many of the aircraft were obsolete, the Russians' heavy tanks, the KV series, were superior to any the Germans threw against them, and the Russian T-34 medium tank was arguably the best tank of the entire war.

German intelligence estimated correctly that Stalin had about 150 divisions in the western Soviet Union, and reckoned that he might be able to muster fifty more. In fact, by the middle of August, Stalin had brought up two hundred fresh divisions. They were badly led, however, as many of their best generals had been killed during the 1930s when Stalin had purged the Soviet Red Army of supposed anti-Communist elements.

In the Baltic states and areas of Ukraine and Belorussia which had been under Soviet Communist rule since 1917, the Germans were greeted as liberators. Even the Jews of Kiev welcomed the Germans, as they had been well treated by the Germans who had invaded Ukraine in World War I. But within days 34,000 Ukrainian Jews had been massacred at Babi Yar, a large ravine to the north of the city. SS death squads also sought out Soviet commissars for execution, and Slavs were summarily killed.

With the invasion of the Soviet Union, Nazi policy towards Jews changed. Instead of imprisoning them or placing them in ghettos, they started killing them – a policy they called the Final Solution of the Jewish Question. Special squads of SS troops followed the advancing German army into the Soviet Union. When they reached a village, they would round up the Jewish residents, march them into the countryside and shoot them. Nazi leaders soon sought a more efficient method of mass

SS soldiers preside over the forced resettlement of Poles at a dispersal camp in Gelsendorf (now in Ukraine)

slaughter, and a method less disturbing for the killers. They began locking captured Jews inside sealed vans and suffocating them on the exhaust fumes as the van was driven to the burial site. By spring 1942, over a million Jews had been killed.

Rapid Progress

Army Group North began its advance from East Prussia. It was to sweep through the Baltic states, then advance towards Leningrad. Despite the swampy, forested terrain and unpaved roads, by 26 June, it had already taken Lithuania and was well into Latvia. That day, the 8th Panzer Division and the 56th Panzer Corps seized the road and rail bridges over the Dvina at Dvinsk (now Daugavpils) and went on to seize the city. After five hours of street fighting, the Germans had crushed all resistance. Three days later, Army Group North had captured Riga, the capital of Latvia, then halted to regroup.

On 3 July, Stalin had rallied sufficiently to make a radio address to the Russian people. He called on their nationalism and announced a 'scorched earth' policy, like the one that had been used against

German troops pause for a meal break in the Russian town of Vitebsk on their way to Moscow, August 1941. On arrival in the town, they found it had been fired by the retreating Soviets

Napoleon's invasion of Russia in 1812. The Germans, Stalin said, must be not be allowed to take 'a single engine, or a single railway truck, and not a pound of bread nor a pint of oil'. The Soviet economy was turned over to war production. Entire factories were moved eastwards, out of the reach of the Germans, and began turning out tanks and aircraft at an astonishing rate.

Both Britain and the United States began supplying the Soviet Union, via the Arctic Ocean to the northern Russian port of Arkhangelsk (Archangel) and through Persia (Iran), which Britain and the Soviet Union jointly occupied.

On 2 July, Army Group North had resumed its offensive. By 20 July it was just 21 miles (34 km) from Leningrad.

Russia had seized parts of Finland under secret protocols of the Molotov–Ribbentrop Pact. But after Barbarossa began, the Finns seized the opportunity to side with Germany. On 10 July, they began their offensive to take back the lands they had lost. By 16 August, they had advanced approximately 60 miles (100 km) along the western shore of Lake Ladoga, cutting Leningrad off from the north.

As the Germans closed on Leningrad from the south, the Red Army suddenly mounted a counter-attack. This gave the population of the city enough time to dig anti-tank trenches and build a defensive perimeter. By 9 September, the Germans had pushed the Red Army back until they were within artillery range of Leningrad. They also began bombing the city. German tanks broke through the last fortified line, but they could make little headway in the narrow streets and the Panzers were withdrawn. But the German infantry and artillery remained to besiege the city.

One million of the city's inhabitants had already been evacuated. The remaining two million were now completely cut off. A siege began that lasted nine hundred days. During that time, Leningrad's only lifeline was across Lake Ladoga, by barge in the summer and by truck and sled across the ice in the winter. When the siege was finally lifted on 19 January 1944, some 200,000 civilians had been killed by the German bombardment and at least 630,000 had perished as a result of starvation and disease.

In the first weeks of Operation Barbarossa, Army Group South quickly overtook most of Ukraine. By

German infantry advance on Leningrad during the latter stages of Barbarossa. The siege of Leningrad would last until the Germans were driven back by the Red Army in 1944

German troops interrogate a Russian peasant. The soldiers in the background wear the metal half-moon badges of the Feldgendarmerie, the Military Police, nicknamed 'headhunters' by ordinary German troops

11 July, it was 10 miles (16 km) from Kiev. With the German army pounding the Russian flanks, Stalin refused his generals' request to pull out of Kiev and on 20 September the Soviet Fifth Army and its Russian armoured column were encircled and captured. Some 520,000 prisoners were taken.

Army Group Centre was the strongest of the three army groups. It consisted of Fourth and Ninth armies, as well as 2nd and 3rd Panzer groups, later redesignated as Panzer armies. Its Panzer and motorized formations burst out from the area north of Warsaw on 22 June, tore huge holes in the Soviet defences and smashed the Soviet forces in Belorussia. Its primary task was to guard Army Group North's right flank as it swept through the Baltic states. Hitler had decreed that only after Leningrad had been captured should Army Group Centre advance on Moscow.

Rapid Advance

Its Panzer spearheads reached Minsk, the capital of Belorussia, on 29 June, encircling four Soviet armies and taking 287,000 prisoners. On 16 July, the German pincers reached Smolensk, 260 miles (420 km) from Moscow, surrounding another large Russian force and taking a further 300,000 prisoners. By July's end, the Germans controlled an area of Soviet territory more than twice the size of France.

By early August, Army Group Centre had covered two-thirds of the distance to Moscow. Feeling that the Red Army could not successfully resist a German advance upon the Soviet capital, von Bock urged the High Command to let him push on to Moscow. But Hitler insisted that taking both Kiev and Leningrad was the priority. He diverted Army Group Centre's forces northwards and southwards to assist, encircling another 665,000 prisoners.

Hitler then gave Bock permission to resume his march on Moscow. But Army Group Centre was not able to regroup and renew the offensive until 2 October. Then it quickly made deep thrusts into the Russian lines, encircling large pockets of Red Army troops at Vyazma and Bryansk. The Vyazma pocket yielded 663,000 prisoners; Bryansk another 100,000. By then, the Russians had only 824 tanks left, no air support and all their massed armies had been lost. The road to Moscow was now open. Foreign diplomats were evacuated and the embalmed body of Lenin, founder of the Soviet Union, had been removed from his tomb in Red Square.

Stalin was about to flee the city, then changed his mind. He imposed martial law and recalled Marshal Georgii Zhukov, his ablest general, from Leningrad to command the defence of Moscow. The Germans were also experiencing severe problems and hardships. The troops were exhausted. The Soviets'

German Panzer IIIs, fitted with armoured skirting to protect their vulnerable tracks, pass through a deserted village in the Soviet Union during the later stages of the invasion

scorched-earth policy had destroyed any housing that could be used as a billet, and their equipment was wearing out. Every advance stretched the German supply lines and, at night, Russian guerrillas would attack the German guards and destroy their supplies.

As October drew on, the weather was changing. Whenever it rained, the roads turned into a sea of mud, and the advance slowed. The German Panzers to the north of Moscow, under the command of General Hermann Hoth, were not able to make a rapid attack through the dense forest there. However, General Guderian's force could attack across the open country to the south. But Zhukov had stationed his last independent tank force, the 4th Armoured Brigade, there. His men were well trained and equipped with T-34 tanks, which had armour that could not be penetrated by the German artillery. Fourth Armoured stopped the German advance almost within sight of Moscow.

Hoth continued to push forward, though. The Russians responded with Katyusha rockets, whose multiple launchers were nicknamed 'Stalin organs' by the Germans, and the Soviet Air Force was airborne again.

The Germans launched their final thrust on Moscow on 15 November. They moved rapidly at first, as the roads were now frozen, and the 7th Panzer Division reached the Moscow-Volga canal, just 20 miles (32 km) from Moscow. On 4 December 1941, the Soviets began a counterattack. Army Group Centre was forced back in spite of Hitler's insistence that it hold its positions regardless of the cost. But the weather had closed in.

The German army was not prepared for the Russian winter. Hitler had been so confident of a quick victory his men had not been issued winter clothing. That winter was the coldest for 140 years.

Boiling soup ladled out from German field kitchens froze within minutes. Axe-shafts splintered when meat was being hacked up and butter had to be cut with a saw. Oil froze in the tanks' engines. Packing grease in the artillery froze and automatic firing mechanisms seized up. By the end of the year there were 100,000 cases of frostbite – over 14,000 were so severe that a limb had to be amputated.

On 7 January 1942, Stalin ordered another offensive. Using the last of his reserves, Zhukov pushed the Germans back and, by the end of January, the front had stabilized some 40 miles (65 km) west of Moscow and the city had been saved.

The Final Solution

Meanwhile, senior Nazi officials gathered at Wannsee in Berlin in January to discuss ways of turning the extermination of the Jews into a more systematic operation. As a result, death camps were built in German-occupied Poland at Belzec, Sobibor, Majdanek, Chelmno, Auschwitz and Treblinka. Here they installed gas chambers disguised as showers. Each camp was capable of killing 15,000 to 25,000 people per day. Mass gassing began at Auschwitz in May 1941.

Throughout occupied Europe, Jews were taken from the ghettos on freight trains to the camps. On arrival, they were examined by an SS doctor, who singled out the able-bodied. The others – some 80 per cent – were stripped of their personal belongings and sent immediately to the gas chambers. Once the prisoners were dead, guards removed any gold teeth from their mouths, then burned their bodies in crematoria. The able-bodied had their heads shaved and belongings confiscated. They were known thereafter by a number tattooed on their arm and were forced to work until too weak to continue, whereupon they were killed or left to die.

Jews found different ways of evading capture or fighting back against the Nazis. Some joined resistance movements in France, Poland and the Soviet Union. Others tried to flee, although this became increasingly difficult as the Nazi reach extended across Europe. A great number went into hiding, and there were many examples of non-Jews risking their lives by offering shelter to Jewish families. Individuals such as Oskar Schindler, a German businessman, and Raoul Wallenburg, a Swedish diplomat, were able to save thousands of Jewish lives by bribing or deceiving Nazi officials. Some Jewish partisan groups, such as Bielski Otriad in Belarus, rescued many Jews from the ghettos.

There were rebellions in several Polish ghettos, including Tuczyn and Marcinkonis. The most significant uprising took place at Warsaw in April–May 1943 when the ghetto was being cleared and the last inmates were sent to the death camps. There were also uprisings at Treblinka and Sobibor death camps in 1943; and in 1944 prisoners rioted at Auschwitz and set fire to the crematorium. These were mostly desperate acts by people who knew they were doomed. Although some managed to escape, the great majority of those who took part were killed.

Besides the death camps, the Nazis operated hundreds of prison camps in Germany and the occupied territories. Conditions in all of them were uniformly harsh and many hundreds of thousands of inmates died of starvation, disease or overwork. In some camps, prisoners died after undergoing cruel medical experiments carried out by Nazi doctors. The Jews were not the only victims of the Holocaust. The Nazis were determined to kill or enslave any they regarded as racially inferior or politically dangerous, including gypsies, Slavs (especially Poles and Soviet prisoners of war), Communists and homosexuals.

Stalingrad

During the winter of 1941, despite the privations of his men on the Eastern Front, Hitler was not downhearted. Most of the Soviet Union's European territory was now in his hands and, by February 1942, the Soviets' winter counterattack had petered out. Hitler now began to make plans to crush the Red Army once and for all. The renewed campaign would attack Stalingrad (now Volgograd), a city that stretched some 30 miles (50 km) along the Volga, 600 miles (1,000 km) south-east of Moscow. It was a huge new industrial city and was paraded as one of the great achievements of the Soviet system. Stalin

A German soldier makes his way around a waterlogged shell crater, Stalingrad, 1942. Six months of fighting has reduced the city to an almost alien landscape

realized that the city that bore his name must be held at all costs. If it fell, so would he.

For Hitler, too, Stalingrad was important. It was a symbol of Communism and had to be crushed. It was also an important centre for the mass production of armaments. Once it had been taken, his victorious army would head up the Volga to encircle Moscow, while a second army would move south-east to take the oilfields of the Caucasus and threaten Turkey and Persia.

However, the war was very different now. The

German army no longer seemed invincible and Hitler infallible. And their brutal treatment of civilians had stiffened resistance.

In the spring of 1942, Stalin made a counterattack in the Kerch Peninsula in the Crimea. This was crushed, and the Germans took 100,000 prisoners. Two fresh Siberian divisions sent to relieve Leningrad were encircled. Then six hundred Russian tanks, two-thirds of the Soviets' force, punched through the Romanian Sixth Army to take Kharkov. But then the Germans counterattacked.

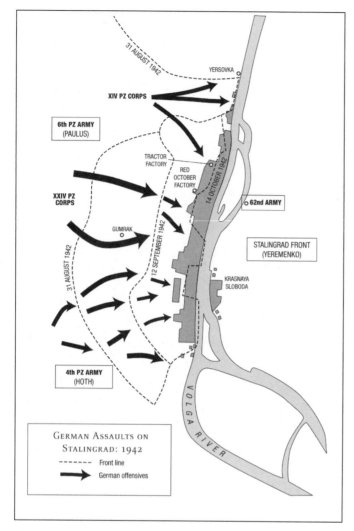

The Battle of Stalingrad, 1942. Both the Red October factory and the tractor factory were held by the Soviets throughout the battle

The Soviets lost nearly a quarter of a million men, along with all their tanks. Now the stage was set for Hitler's summer offensive.

On 28 June, on a wide front stretching from Kursk to Rostov, the Panzers went roaring across the open steppes. The dust pall they kicked up could be seen for 40 miles (65 km), and it was soon joined by smoke from burning villages. There were no significant forces to oppose them as they headed for Stalingrad.

Stalin then made the decision to commit the

Moscow reserve to the defence of Stalingrad and the desperate race to get them there began. Despite stiff opposition, on 22 August, German troops reached the Volga, within mortar range of a vital railway bridge. Between 25 and 29 August, the German 6th Army under General Friedrich Paulus made a ferocious attempt to storm the city before the reinforcements could arrive.

Terror bombing sent the civilian population fleeing to the other side of the Volga and the authorities began evacuating the factories. When Stalin heard of this, he stopped the evacuations. Workers in the tractor factory continued producing new tanks and armoured cars until the Germans were on their doorstep. Then they would sling ammunition belts over their overalls and take up their positions.

The Germans were the masters of the Blitzkrieg. They were not used to slow, grinding, man-to-man fighting through the rubble of a ruined city. The Russians, by contrast, quickly learned to adapt their tactics to the new situation, and every move the Germans made cost them dearly. After weeks of ceaseless fighting against crack German troops, the Red Army still held a 9-mile (14-km) strip along the banks of the Volga.

On 12 September, Hitler authorized a new offensive. The following day, Paulus sent in three Panzer divisions backed by eight divisions of infantry. Against them, the Soviets had forty tanks, all but nineteen immobile. The Sixty-Second Army had been reduced to just three infantry divisions, the remnants of four others and two battle-damaged tank brigades. And there were no reserves, as every man had already been thrown into the battle. The Soviet headquarters, however, were on the spot. General Vasili Chuikov had made the dangerous crossing of the Volga and had set up his command

post in a dugout, by the river near Pushkin Street bridge. With their backs to the river, his men were inspired by these words from Chuikov: 'There is no land across the Volga.' For those who did not get the message, there were firing squads to deal with the deserters. Hundreds were shot.

Vital Link

The Germans flung themselves at the middle of the Russian line and, on the afternoon of 14 September, they broke through and seized Mamayev Hill. From the high ground there, they could concentrate artillery fire on the vital ferry link across the Volga. The 76th Infantry Division overwhelmed the defenders at a ruined hospital in the middle of the Soviet line. Victory now seemed certain, and many Germans got drunk on looted vodka. The only resistance now seemed to be snipers.

That night, the fighting came within 200 yards (180 m) of Chuikov's headquarters, and staff officers joined the fight. On the night of 14 September, Russian Guardsmen had to scramble ashore under fire. There was no possibility of them counterattacking as a coherent division, and they were soon dispersed among the ruins in isolated pockets with no intercommunication.

The street fighting had also broken up the German formations. They now fought through the devastated streets in small battle groups comprising three or four Panzers and a company of German infantrymen, which had to laboriously clear each pocket individually. Russian riflemen and machine-gunners hid in ruined buildings, craters and behind mountains of rubble. They waited until the Panzers had gone by, then attacked the infantry. And in the narrow streets, the Panzers were very vulnerable both to grenades dropped from directly

above and to anti-tank guns. The battle hinged on house-to-house combat fought with bullet, grenade, bayonet and flame-thrower.

The Germans found that it took a whole day and numerous casualties to take 200 yards (180 m). Even then, the Russians reappeared at night, knocking holes in attic walls so that they could reoccupy buildings over the heads of the Germans. Despite that, victory seemed near. A German salient ran

> *But it did not seem to matter how much of the city the Germans occupied. The Russians would not give up. Pockets of Guardsmen and Russian Marines repelled wave after wave of attackers*

down the Tsarita tributary to the Volga itself. But it did not seem to matter how much of the city the Germans occupied. The Russians would not give up. Although bombed and blasted, the grain elevators there still stood defiant. They were occupied by pockets of Guardsmen and Russian Marines who repelled wave after wave of attackers.

For the Germans, two months of fighting for a narrow strip of the ruined city of Stalingrad was a propaganda disaster. The German people were told that the Russians were throwing wave after wave of men into the battle and were exhausting their reserves. In fact, the opposite was true. During September and October, the Germans threw no fewer than nineteen newly formed armoured brigades and twenty-seven infantry divisions into the battle.

Meanwhile Zhukov sent only the bare minimum needed to hold off the Germans, so that he

German field gun in action during the fighting for Stalingrad, winter 1942

could build up strength for a counterattack.

As Russian artillery fire grew steadily heavier, the nights began to draw in and the Germans began to fear that they would be spending another winter in Russia. Quickly Paulus planned a fourth all-out offensive and Hitler publicly promised that Stalingrad would fall 'very shortly'.

Forty thousand Russians now held a strip of the city barely 10 miles (16 km) long. At its widest, it reached one and a quarter miles (2 km) inland from the west bank of the Volga; at its narrowest, it was about 500 yards (450 m). The Russians defending it, however, were hardened troops who knew every cellar, sewer and ruin of this wasteland. They watched German advances through periscopes and cut them down with machine-gun fire. Snipers stalked the cratered streets, or lay camouflaged and silent for hours on end awaiting their prey. Against them were pitched veteran German troops, who were demoralized by the losses they had taken, or raw recruits, who could be in no way prepared for the horrors they were about to face.

On 4 October, the Germans were about to launch their offensive when the Russians counterattacked in the area around the tractor factory. This threw the Germans off balance. Although little ground was lost, it cost them many casualties. The Luftwaffe sent in eight hundred dive-bombers, and the German artillery pounded the city mercilessly. After a five-hour bombardment, which shattered glass deep below ground and killed sixty-one men in Chuikov's headquarters, the German attack eventually went ahead.

Killing Grounds

On 14 October, two new armoured divisions and five infantry divisions pushed forward on a front just 3 miles (5 km) wide. They found themselves lured into special killing grounds the Russians had prepared, where houses and sometimes whole blocks or squares had been heavily mined. Combat became so close that the Germans would occupy one half of a shattered building, while the Russians occupied the other. When the Russians prepared a building as a stronghold, they would destroy the stairs so that the Germans would have to fight for each floor independently. That day, 14 October, according to Chuikov, was 'the bloodiest and most ferocious day of the whole battle'.

The Soviets were pushed back so close to the Volga that boats bringing supplies across the Volga came under heavy machine gun fire. At the last moment a Siberian division was put in. Its men were told to fight to the death. They were pounded with mortars, artillery, and dive bombers. Over the next two weeks the Germans made 117 separate attacks – twenty-three on a single day. But the Siberians held out. Stalled, the Germans took to the sewers for the last three hundred yards under the city to the Volga. But when they reached it, they were cut off. There was hand-to-hand combat under the rubble, both sides high on vodka and Benzedrine. After four days, only Russians were left. Then a terrible silence fell over Stalingrad – the silence of death.

By that time, Zhukov had built up a new army. Guns opened up to the north and south of the city. A pincer movement quickly encircled 250,000 Germans in the most decisive breakthrough on the Eastern Front. Hitler told Paulus to hold his ground until 'Fortress Stalingrad' was relieved. Göring told Hitler that his Luftwaffe could fly in 500 tons of stores a day. Meanwhile General Erich von Manstein rushed to the rescue with a spearhead

Lines of German troops march into captivity after the Soviet recapture of Stalingrad, February 1943. Almost 90,000 German soldiers were taken prisoner after the battle; few were to see their homeland again

of Panzers, leading a convoy of supply trucks. He was halted by Russian T-34s and Paulus refused to try to break out as Hitler had ordered him to stay where he was. Göring failed to live up to his promise. On 8 January, the Russians offered terms. Hitler promoted Paulus Field Marshal to pressure him not to accept. On 30 January, Paulus's command post was overrun and 91,000 frozen and hungry survivors were captured. As they were marched away a Soviet colonel pointed at the rubble of Stalingrad and shouted: 'That's how Berlin is going to look.' Two entire German armies were wiped out including their reserves. Some 300,000 trained men had been lost. They were irreplaceable. The battle had been a blood bath. In the final stages alone, 147,200 Germans and 46,700 Russians had been killed.

Chapter 5

WAR IN THE PACIFIC

At 0753 hours on Sunday, 7 December 1941, 181 Japanese warplanes attacked the US Pacific Fleet as it lay at anchor in Pearl Harbor, the great US naval base on Oahu in the Hawaiian Islands. Forty minutes later, a second wave of 170 planes staged a second attack. While there had been no formal declaration, the fact that the United States was now at war was inescapable.

Brewing Conflict

Although the attack at Pearl Harbor was a surprise, a war between the United States and Japan had not been entirely unexpected. In the early twentieth century, Japan had risen to become a great naval power, beating the great Russian Imperial Fleet in the Russo-Japanese War of 1904–05. In the 1930s, militarists gained the upper hand in the government. Already the Japanese held Korea and Manchuria,

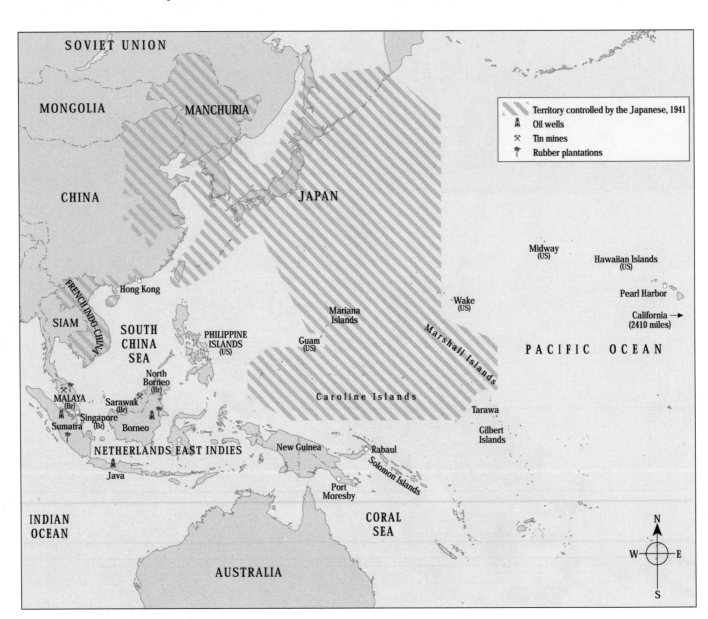

The Pacific Theatre 1941–45

Aerial view of Ford Island during the Japanese surprise attack on Pearl Harbor, Hawaii. A plume of water rises from an explosion, as several planes swoop over the island

and, in 1937, they attacked China. To add to their growing possessions on the mainland, they aimed to take over the British, French and Dutch colonies in the Far East, along with the Philippines, which was under US control, and establish what Japan called a 'Greater East Asia Co-Prosperity Sphere' – in other words, a Japanese empire.

Washington backed Chiang Kai-shek, the Chinese nationalist leader who was resisting the Japanese onslaught, and imposed sanctions on Japan. The Japanese joined the Axis and signed the Tripartite Pact with the Germans and Italy on 27 September 1940.

When Hitler attacked the Soviet Union in June 1941, he invited Japan to join the war and seize Russia's eastern seaboard. But Japan had been soundly defeated by the Soviets at the Battle of Nomonhan in Mongolia in 1939, weeks before the Germans attacked Poland, and decided to benefit from the German attack, rather than aid it. Operation Barbarossa effectively neutralized the Soviet Union as an enemy in the Far East, and it presented the Japanese with the opportunity to attack to the south and seize the European colonies there – provided any threat from the United States could be neutralized as well.

On 20 November 1941, America received an ultimatum from the Japanese government, saying that the United States must withdraw its support from the Chinese government, lift its trade embargo and supply Japan with the one vital commodity it lacked – oil.

The United States could not comply. Any concession to the Japanese would mean that China would fall, along with British possessions in the Far East. Without its Empire, Britain would fall, leaving the whole of Europe, Africa, and Asia to the Axis.

America would then be surrounded on all sides by hostile dictatorships.

On 26 November, Washington sent a reply to the Japanese ultimatum that simply outlined the principles of self-determination once more. The United States knew that this would not be acceptable to the Japanese, but it did not know that the Japanese fleet had already sailed.

The man who had drawn up the plan for the attack on Pearl Harbor was the Commander in Chief of the Japanese Imperial Navy, Admiral

Japanese attack on 'Battleship Row', seen from a Japanese aircraft. Torpedo drop splashes and running tracks are visible at left and centre. White smoke in the distance is from Hickam Field. Grey smoke in the centre middle distance is from the torpedoed USS *Helena*

Isoroku Yamamoto. He believed that Japan could not win a war with the United States. Asked about Japan's chances of victory, Yamamoto replied, 'If I am told to fight regardless of the consequences, I shall run wild for the first six months or a year, but I have absolutely no confidence about the second and third years.'

Outside Bet

The Japanese government gambled that six months was enough. In that time, its forces could sweep through Southeast Asia and seize the Indonesian oilfields and enough raw materials to supply its industry for a prolonged war.

The Japanese navy had realized that aircraft carriers, not battleships, would be the crucial weapon in a war in the Pacific. It had built a carrier fleet and equipped it with dive-bombers, torpedo bombers and fighters that were the best in the world. Yamamoto's plan was to knock out the US Pacific Fleet at Pearl Harbor in an attack so swift that it would have no time to react.

While increasingly hostile diplomatic traffic was exchanged between Washington and Tokyo, Yamamoto secretly massed an armada under Vice Admiral Chuichi Nagumo in the Kurile Islands to the north-east of Japan. There were six huge aircraft carriers – the *Akagi*, *Kaga*, *Hiryu*, *Soryu*, *Shokaku* and *Zuikaku* – carrying 423 warplanes between them. They set sail on 26 November.

The fleet took a northerly route, staying out of the shipping lanes, and maintained radio silence. It arrived in position north-east of the Hawaiian Islands on 6 December. That day, the government in Tokyo began sending a long message to the Japanese embassy in Washington, D.C. This brought diplomatic negotiations to a conclusion,

although it fell short of a declaration of war. But delay in decoding such a long letter meant that it was not delivered until after the attack had begun.

When the Japanese fleet sailed, it was thought that all six US aircraft carriers were in Pearl Harbor. Five had been, but the *Hornet* and the *Yorktown* had been transferred to the Atlantic, while the *Saratoga* had been pulled back to protect the United States' West Coast. And, on 28 November, the *Enterprise* and the *Lexington* set sail westwards to deliver planes to Wake Island and Midway.

At 0550 on the morning of 7 December, the Japanese carriers turned into the wind. Conditions were far from perfect. The wind was gusting and the sea was high, but only one of the 183 planes in the first wave was lost on take-off. Another developed engine trouble and had to turn back. But by 0620, forty-nine bombers, fifty-one dive-bombers, forty torpedo planes and forty-one Zero fighters were heading to Oahu, while the second wave was being marshalled on the flight deck.

At 0700, Commander Mitsui Fuchida, the attack force flight leader, picked up music from a Hawaiian radio station and locked onto it. Five minutes later, two American radar operators in the newly established US military radar station on the north of Oahu spotted a blip, but a flight of American B-17s was expected from the mainland that morning.

The Japanese planes stayed above a thick layer of cloud. It was Sunday morning and few navy men were on deck. The ships were moored close together, making them an easy target. Of the three hundred planes based at the airfields on the island, only three were airborne, with those on the ground parked in close formation.

At 0753, Fuchida sent the famous radio message 'Tora, Tora, Tora' – 'Tiger, Tiger, Tiger' – which meant that the Americans had been taken completely by surprise. And the Japanese planes went in for the kill.

Under Attack

When the first bomb dropped, the Americans who heard it assumed that it had been dropped by accident by one of their own planes. It was only when a dive-bomber blew up a hangar at the Ford Island Command Center that Commander Logan Ramsey realized that the island was under attack. Frantically, he sent the radio message, 'Air raid, Pearl Harbor. This is no drill.'

When the first bomb dropped, the Americans assumed it had been dropped by accident by one of their own planes. It was only when a dive-bomber blew up a hangar, they realized the island was under attack

By 0755 hours, the Pacific Fleet and the surrounding airfields were under full-scale attack. For the next two hours, bombs rained down and torpedoes sliced through the unprotected hulls of the US Navy's prize battleships. Amid the explosions gunners managed to return fire, but they were hampered by firing from capsizing decks and a shortage of ammunition which was locked in storage boxes.

The battleship USS *Arizona* blew up and was completely destroyed. The *Oklahoma* capsized. The *California*, *Nevada* and *West Virginia* sank at their moorings. Three other battleships, three cruisers, three destroyers, and several other vessels also suffered damage. Some 169 aircraft were completely destroyed and 150 damaged, mainly on the ground. In all, some 2,403 Americans were killed, including sixty-eight civilians. Another 1,176 were wounded.

The Japanese lost 29 planes. Another ten or fifteen made it back to their carriers, but were so badly damaged they were pushed overboard to make room for incoming planes. Around another forty were damaged but repairable. It seemed an overwhelming victory. However, despite the pleadings of Fuchida, Admiral Nagumo had refused to send in a third wave of planes already fuelled, loaded with bombs and waiting on the flight decks. With the defences at Pearl now crippled, a third or fourth wave could have finished off the battleships and put the airfields out of action. And an attack on the US Navy fuel depot would have sent the United States' complete naval strategy for the Pacific up in smoke.

To pick up incoming planes, the Japanese fleet had sailed to within 190 miles (300 km) of the island and was now vulnerable. Nagumo did not know where the US carrier fleet was, but by now it would be looking for them. He had fulfilled his mission. According to the damage reports he had been receiving, the US Pacific Fleet would be out of action for at least six months, which was all that was required. So Nagumo's flagship, the *Akagi*, hoisted the signal flag ordering a withdrawal to the northwest. Below decks, the disappointed pilots said, 'Now we can live to be a hundred.'

The following day, President Roosevelt addressed a joint session of the US Congress: 'Yesterday, December 7, 1941 – a day which will live in infamy – the United States of America was suddenly and deliberately attacked by the naval and air forces of the Empire of Japan.'

Pearl Harbor was not the only target that came under attack by the Japanese. President Roosevelt went on to list what else had happened on that day: 'Yesterday the Japanese government also launched an attack against Malaya. Last night Japanese forces attacked Hong Kong. Last night Japanese forces attacked Guam. Last night Japanese forces attacked the Philippine Islands. Last night the Japanese attacked Wake Island. This morning the Japanese attacked Midway Island. I ask that Congress declare that, since the unprovoked and dastardly attack by Japan on Sunday, December 7th, a state of war has existed between the United States and the Japanese Empire.'

At 1610 that afternoon, 8 December, President Roosevelt signed the declaration of war. That same day, Britain also declared war on Japan.

For the Japanese, the attacks on Hong Kong and Singapore were particularly gratifying, as Britain was seen as Japan's real enemy in the Far East. The following day, the Japanese occupied Bangkok and landed on Tarawa and Makin in the Gilbert Islands. Then, on 10 December, Britain's two most powerful warships east of Suez – the battleship *Prince of Wales* and the cruiser *Repulse* – steaming to the defence of Singapore, were sunk in the Gulf of Siam. That same day, the Japanese landed on the main Philippine island of Luzon.

On 11 December 1941, Hitler made perhaps the biggest blunder of the war. He declared war on the United States. He was not obliged to do that under the Tripartite Pact, just as Japan had failed to declare war on the Soviet Union.

Roosevelt already had an agreement with Churchill that, apart from defensive actions in the Pacific, they would pursue the war in Europe first. But the American public was baying for blood. Admiral Chester W. Nimitz was appointed commander of the Pacific Fleet. He assembled the three carriers that had been out to sea when the Japanese had attacked – the USS *Lexington*, *Saratoga* and *Enterprise*. Along with five others – the *Langley*, *Ranger*, *Wasp*, *Hornet* and *Yorktown*, these would be the backbone of the US fleet that fought the Pacific war.

> *On 11 December 1941, Hitler made perhaps the biggest blunder of the war. He declared war on the United States. He was not obliged to do that under the Tripartite Pact...*

The Doolittle Raid

On 18 April 1942, 16 B-25 bombers under the command of Lieutenant Colonel James Doolittle, each carrying one ton of bombs, took off from the USS *Hornet* and set out for Japan, some 600 miles (965 km) away. Hopes that the ship could get closer were dashed when the carrier unexpectedly encountered Japanese patrol boats. The small boats were sunk, but not before warnings about the approaching American force had been radioed back.

Rather than abandon the raid, it was brought forward. The cities hit included Tokyo, Kobe and Yokohama. The intention was then to fly on to China, which had been at war with Japan for some five years. But due to fuel shortage one of the planes came down near Vladivostock and its crew was interned by the Russians who were not yet at war with Japan. They escaped in 1943. Two planes and eight men fell into Japanese hands. Although they were prisoners of war, three were shot. Another died of malnutrition while in captivity. Two men drowned after their plane came down in the sea. However, a large percentage of the crew survived, although some suffered serious injuries.

Although damage to Japan was slight the high command had told the people that the homeland would not be bombed. To push the Americans back out of bombing range, Yamamoto insisted that they take the Midway Islands.

The Battle of the Coral Sea

The first stand-off between the Japanese and US navies occurred at the Battle of the Coral Sea on 7 and 8 May 1942. By monitoring enemy communications, the Americans discovered their plan to capture Port Moresby, on New Guinea's south-eastern coast, threatening Australia.

As a result the Japanese aircraft carriers *Shokaku* and *Zuikaku* were confronted by the USS

Lieutenant Colonel James H. Doolittle, of the US Army Air Force, wires a Japanese medal to a 500-pound bomb, shortly before his force of sixteen B-25B bombers took off for Japan on what became known as the Doolittle Raid, 18 April 1942

Lexington and the USS *Yorktown*. The ships never came closer than 70 miles (112 km) and the battle was fought by carrier-borne aircraft for the first time.

On 7 May 1942 Japanese spy planes reported seeing a carrier and a cruiser, and a force of attack aircraft was dispatched. They were, in fact, a US oil cargo ship and an escorting destroyer. Both were wrecked by enemy action.

America dished out similar treatment to a light carrier, *Shoho*, and four cruisers. The Japanese had no idea where the American planes had come from.

The following day the *Lexington* was torpedoed and bombed. Abandoned she sank. The *Yorktown* was also badly damaged and had to withdraw. Meanwhile American planes wreaked damage on *Shokaku* and she departed for safer waters. Many more Japanese aircraft were lost than American. But benefiting from low cloud cover, the *Zuikaku* was undamaged.

So the battle was a marginal victory for the Japanese, though they pulled out, leaving the field to the Americans.

The Battle of Midway

The Midway Islands, measuring just two square miles (5 sq. km), sit squarely in the Pacific Ocean, and were unpopulated except for US military personnel. It was a second string naval base after Pearl Harbor.

Admiral Yamamoto envisaged a swift invasion to oust the Americans and take the airfield. He also believed that this would entice US aircraft carriers into action, where they could be destroyed by a superior Japanese strike force. For good measure,

he planned to capture the Aleutian Islands, which were US territory, to distract American forces.

Code breakers knew an operation was planned but they were unsure of the target. Commander Joseph P. Rochefort, in charge of intelligence, asked the base at Midway to broadcast a bogus message, claiming that its desalination plant was out of order. Then Japanese coded traffic revealed the target was having problems with fresh water. US carriers, including the freshly repaired *Yorktown*, moved into position.

Dauntless dive bombers from USS *Hornet* approaching the already fatally damaged Japanese heavy cruiser *Mikuma* in the third set of attacks on her, during the early afternoon of 6 June 1942

Japanese heavy cruiser *Mikuma*, during the afternoon of 6 June 1942, after she had been bombed by planes from USS *Enterprise* and *Hornet*

At dawn on 4 June 1942 both sides sent out spotter planes. The American pilots came across the Japanese naval force as expected. But the Japanese were concentrating on the military strength of Midway. Only later did they discover the presence of the American fleet.

Although the airbase escaped largely unscathed, the tally of hits against US aircraft by Zero fighters was immense.

The Mitsubishi A6M 'Zero' fighter was the pride of the Japanese fleet. It worked in conjunction with the Aichi D3A dive bomber, known as 'Val' to the Allies, and the Nakajima B5N otherwise known as 'Kate', an attack aircraft carrying an 18-inch torpedo or a 1,757-pound armour-piercing bomb. All were ferried into position by the three carrier fleets.

It was not until 10.25 am – some four hours after the first skirmishes over Midway – that significant headway was forged by the Americans. Three squadrons of scout bombers – two from the *Enterprise* and one from the *Yorktown* – targeted the four carriers whose decks were by now full of refuelled and fully-armed aircraft. In a matter of moments the carriers *Akagi*, *Kaga* and *Soryu* were blazing and crippled. Only *Hiryu* remained operational.

Eighteen dive bombers escorted by six fighters sought out the *Yorktown* about ninety minutes later and wreaked havoc with three bombs scoring direct hits. A second attack wave against the *Yorktown* mounted by the Japanese caused further damage and she had to be abandoned. Two days later a torpedo from a Japanese submarine sent her to the bottom.

However, US carrier planes went after *Hiryu* once more and inflicted significant damage. Fires raged out of control and *Hiryu*'s crew ultimately had to abandon ship. On board, Admiral Yamaguchi and Captain Kaku committed suicide. Within a few hours Yamamoto abandoned the Midway operation. The Japanese took two tiny islands in the Aleutians but the Imperial Japanese Navy had lost four heavy carriers, one heavy cruiser, a hundred pilots, 3,400 sailors, three carrier captains and an admiral. The Americans also salvaged the wreckage of a Zero for experts to work out its weak points. American losses amounted to one carrier, a destroyer and 150 planes. It was six months after Pearl Harbor and the battle for mastery of the Pacific had turned in favour of America.

Norman Bel Geddes' diorama, depicting the torpedoing of USS *Hammann* and USS *Yorktown* by Japanese submarine I-168, on the afternoon of 6 June 1942, during the Battle of Midway

Chapter 6

THE SOFT UNDERBELLY

At the conference in Casablanca in January 1943, Churchill persuaded Roosevelt that the Allies' next move should be to attack the 'soft underbelly' of Europe. At this point in the war, Italy was looking particularly weak. When Mussolini had mobilized on 10 June 1940, he had seventy-five divisions. Twenty more had been raised, but twenty-seven had been lost in Africa. The Italian Eighth Army had been sent to join Hitler's 'crusade against Bolshevism' in the Soviet Union. Thirty-six Italian divisions were fighting guerrillas in the Balkans or occupying France. In three years, more than a third of Mussolini's army had been lost.

In 1943, only thirty divisions were available to defend the homeland – and some of those were not combat ready. Only twenty were available to face an Allied invasion. Along with the regular army there were 'coastal defence' units, which were the Italian equivalent of the Home Guard. Although there were twenty-one divisions and five brigades, they were largely manned by old men. They were poorly equipped with weaponry that came from the Vichy French army disbanded in 1942. Weapons often came with parts missing or without ammunition. The coastal defence units were also strung out along Italy's long coastline. In Sicily, there were just forty-one men per mile. This was not a force that could repel a determined Allied invasion.

The problem was that, to the Allies, it seemed blindingly obvious to anyone who could read a map that their next move would be the invasion of Sicily. However, two members of the XX – 'double cross' – Committee, Squadron Leader Sir Archibald Cholmondley and Lieutenant Commander

Il Duce (Mussolini) addresses his troops from the top of an Italian light tank

(Ewen Montagu, came up with a cunning plan. They would deliver forged documents into German hands, showing the Allies were going to attack Sardinia. A body carrying the documents would be dropped by submarine off the coast of Spain, where the Fascist government worked closely with the Abwehr, German military intelligence. The corpse could then credibly be that of a courier as he would not have been lost flying over enemy territory.

Operation Mincemeat, as it became known, worked perfectly. Hitler ordered the strengthening of fortifications on Sardinia and neighbouring Corsica, and he sent an additional Waffen SS brigade to Sardinia. One Panzer division was sent from France to Greece. Another two Panzer divisions were sent from Russia, immediately before the great tank battle at Kursk. And Rommel was posted to Athens to form an army group. Indications of the Allies' true intentions came

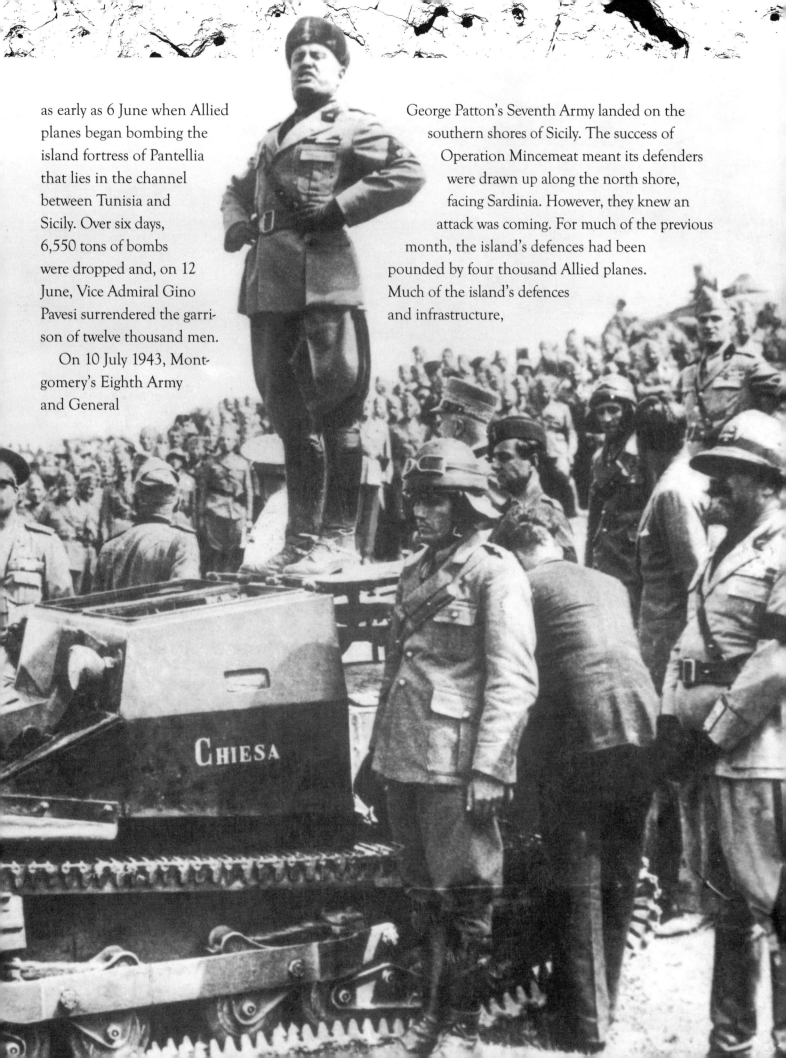

as early as 6 June when Allied planes began bombing the island fortress of Pantellia that lies in the channel between Tunisia and Sicily. Over six days, 6,550 tons of bombs were dropped and, on 12 June, Vice Admiral Gino Pavesi surrendered the garrison of twelve thousand men.

On 10 July 1943, Montgomery's Eighth Army and General George Patton's Seventh Army landed on the southern shores of Sicily. The success of Operation Mincemeat meant its defenders were drawn up along the north shore, facing Sardinia. However, they knew an attack was coming. For much of the previous month, the island's defences had been pounded by four thousand Allied planes. Much of the island's defences and infrastructure,

Zero Hour: the start of the Allied invasion of Sicily – zero hour has arrived and the men of the Allied forces receive the word 'Go'

including the airfields, had been wiped out.

Even so, Operation Husky nearly turned into a disaster. The previous evening, Axis aircraft had spotted the Allied fleet leaving Malta. That night the armada was hit by a storm and was nearly forced to turn back. However, because of the heavy weather, the defenders dropped their guard. But high winds took their toll on the airborne troops, blowing gliders and parachutists out to sea to their deaths. Those that landed on the island at around five o'clock in the morning were widely dispersed. Nevertheless they succeeded in harassing the enemy's movements and around a hundred British airborne troops took a vital bridge at Primsole south of Catania and held it for five days until the Eighth Army arrived to relieve them.

Operation Husky

At dawn on the 10th, the coastal defences were attacked by tactical aircraft and pounded by naval gunfire. Then a fleet of 2,590 ships, including 237 troop transports and 1,742 landing craft began putting ashore 115,000 British and Canadian troops and 66,000 Americans. Facing them were the 230,000 men and 150 guns of the Italian Sixth Army, who had few motorized units, supported by the 15th Panzergrenadier Division, which was only partially motorized, and the 'Hermann Göring' Panzer Division, which had only two battalions of infantry and less than a hundred tanks – though these did include a company of Tigers. There was also a division and a brigade of the coastal defence force holding 120 miles (190 km) of the south coast against six British and American divisions, while to the west of Licata the American 3rd Division were opposed by just two battalions.

The Italian coastal defence force put up a heroic defence. But facing superior numbers supported by tanks they were virtually wiped out. By the evening, the commander of the Italian Sixth Army, General Alfredo Guzzoni ordered the 15th Panzergrenadier Division to hold the central town of Enna, while the 'Hermann Göring' Panzer Division and the Italian 'Livorno' Division attacked the American bridgehead at Gela.

The following morning the Panzers ran into the forward posts of the American 1st Division, but once they got within two thousand yards of the beach they came under fire from six destroyers and the cruisers *Savannah* and *Boise*, who loosed off 3,194 five- and six-inch shells, knocking out thirty tanks. The 'Livorno' Division was also badly mauled. Meanwhile the British Eighth Army occupied the ports of Augusta and Syracuse without a shot being fired as their garrisons had already been evacuated.

On 14 July, the British Eighth Army and American Seventh Army met up. Montgomery then planned a dash up the east coast to Messina, trapping the defenders on the island and forcing a surrender, but Field Marshal Albert Kesselring, the German commander in chief in Italy, pre-empted him. He sent in the 29th Panzergrenadier Division and two parachute regiments. And on 17 July, General Hans Hube and the staff of XIV Panzer Corps took over command of all German fighting forces in Sicily. Resistance stiffened and Montgomery was stopped at Catania. He then turned inland, switching his attack to the west of Mount Etna.

The following morning the Panzers ran into the forward posts of the American 1st Division, but once they got within two thousand yards of the beach they came under fire from six destroyers...

Hemmed In

Patton pushed westwards and captured Sicily's capital Palermo on 22 July. He, too, planned a dash on Messina along the north coast. But Hube stopped him at the little town of Santo Stefano, halfway down the coast road. Meanwhile the 1st Canadian Division bypassed Enna and pushed north-west, confining the defenders to the north-east corner of the island. The British were now landing the 78th Division at Syracuse, while the American 9th Division landed at Palermo. This brought the Allies' strength up to eleven divisions. Totally outnumbered, Hube pulled back.

The Italians had already suffered a series of defeats in North Africa and, with the mainland of Italy now under threat, they were eager to make peace with the Allies. On the night of 24 July 1943, the Fascist Grand Council voted Mussolini from power. The following day, he was arrested and imprisoned at Campo Imperatore high in the Abruzzi mountains, where it was thought rescue was impossible. Meanwhile the new Italian government began secret peace talks with the Allies.

A few days after the fall of Mussolini, Kesselring was ordered to withdraw the four divisions of the XIV Panzer Corps from Sicily. The Strait of Messina was bristling with anti-aircraft guns and Hube managed to get two-thirds of his force across. Three hours later, the British and Americans met in the ruins of Messina. There was now just two miles of clear water between the Allied army and the mainland of Italy.

The cost of Operation Husky was 5,532 Allied dead, 14,410 wounded and 2,869 missing. The Italians lost 4,278 dead and the Germans 4,325. The Allies had taken some 132,000 prisoners, along with 520 guns and 260 tanks.

The Invasion of Italy

On 2 September 1943, a small Allied force had landed on the 'heel' of Italy, quickly taking the ports of Brindisi and Taranto. The following day Montgomery's Eighth Army crossed the Strait of Messina and landed in Calabria, on the 'toe' of Italy. That day, the new Italian government agreed to the Allied peace terms.

Under the peace agreement, the Americans had promised to land the 82nd Airborne Division on the outskirts of Rome and take over the city, but the 3rd Panzergrenadier Division got there first.

Salerno

On 9 September an Anglo-American force under General Mark Clark landed at Salerno, 30 miles (50 km) south of Naples. Kesselring had anticipated this and managed to hold the Allies back in their bridgehead for six days.

Seventeen more divisions were sent into Italy under the command of Rommel, who established his headquarters in Bologna. Several Italian units melted away, but Rommel managed to take over ten divisions and add them to his command.

To give his takeover of Italy some sort of legitimacy, Hitler hatched a plot to rescue Mussolini. On 12 September 1943, German commandos under the command of SS officer Otto Skorzeny crash-landed gliders on the slopes behind Campo Imperatore and freed him. Mussolini was flown to Munich, where Hitler suggested he set up a new Fascist republic in north Italy. The Repubblica Sociale Italiana was established on 18 September at Salò on Lake Garda.

Also on 12 September Kesselring counter-attacked. He concentrated his attack between the British 56th Division on the right and the American 45th Division on the left, which had made quicker progress. The German forces attempted then to encircle the Americans and crush the beachhead at Salerno. The battle hinged around Ponte Bruciato. Clark threw every man he had into the fight, including a regimental band and the headquarters orderlies and cooks. However, the German advance foundered when Hitler refused to reinforce Kesselring's Tenth Army after Rommel had advised him that Italy could not be defended south of a line from La Spezia to Rimini.

At Salerno, the Germans were stopped 5 miles (8 km) from the beach, where they were pinned

Salerno Landing: Allied troops land at Salerno, south of Naples, 9 September 1943

down by Allied naval bombardment. New German radio-controlled bombs hit the American cruiser *Savannah* as well as the British cruiser *Uganda* and the battleship *Warspite*. Eventually the Americans were relieved when Montgomery broke through at Agropoli. The German Tenth Army had been defeated at a cost of 5,674 American casualties.

On 1 October the American Fifth Army entered Naples, while more British forces landed at Bari and Termoli on the Adriatic coast. Then on 13 October 1943, the Italian government in Rome declared war on Germany. This did not bother Kesselring unduly as German reinforcements were already consolidating their hold on north and central Italy. Rommel's Panzers managed to check the American Fifth Army on the Volturno River, just 20 miles (32 km) north of Naples, then held them on the Garigliano. However, Rommel was still urging that Germany abandon Rome and withdraw to the north. On 21 November he was relieved and Kesselring was left in sole command.

On the east coast, the British Eighth Army was stopped on the Sangro River. The advance had run out of steam because the roads, which ran through mountainous terrain, were jammed with vehicles. So the French landed the 2nd Moroccan Division and the 3rd Algerian Division with 65,000 men and 2,500 horses and mules. The 2nd Moroccan Division proved its worth the first time it came under fire, earning the French Expeditionary Corps a place in the line.

Anzio

The Germans dug in along the Gustav Line, a defensive position that ran for a hundred miles across the Italian peninsula, which pivoted on the town of Cassino with the historic monastery of Monte Cassino on the mountain above it.

The road to Rome now blocked, the Allies staged another amphibious assault, landing 70,000 troops at Anzio and nearby Nettuno just 37 miles (60 km) south of Rome and 60 miles (97 km) behind the Gustav Line on 22 January 1944. The landings were initially successful but the American commander Major General John P. Lucas did not seize the opportunity to make a dash for Rome, cutting German communications on the way and forcing Kesselring to evacuate the Gustav Line. Instead, Lucas took the best part of a week to consolidate his bridgehead. This gave time for Kesselring to mount a counter-offensive, effectively trapping the huge Anglo-American force in their bridgehead. In frustration, Churchill wrote to Alexander who was in overall command in Italy: 'I expected to see a wild cat roaring into the mountains – and what do I find? A whale wallowing on the beaches.'

Churchill felt that if the landings at Anzio and

Nettuno had worked, his whole 'soft underbelly' strategy would prove itself and Anglo-American forces would be able to drive up the Italian peninsula, through Austria into Germany before the Red Army got there.

Unable to move, Lucas was forced to establish a static defence, which was pounded by a 28cm rail gun, known variously as 'Anzio Annie' or the 'Anzio Express'. As the landings at Anzio and Nettuno had failed to outflank the Gustav Line, a breakthrough

Field Marshal 'Smiling Albert' Kesselring, in conversation with German troops in Italy

was imperative. The New Zealand Corps were order to lead an attack up the Liri Valley. Its commander Lieutenant-General Bernard Freyberg insisted that the historic monastery of Monte Cassino, which overlooked it, be bombed before his men advanced.

Monte Cassino

On the morning of 15 February 1944, 229 American bombers dropped 453 tons of incendiaries and high explosives on the monastery, reducing it to rubble. However, this did not lead to the breakthrough the Allies craved. So on 15 March, 775 planes dropped 1,250 tons of bombs on the small town of Cassino, which was also shelled for two hours. But this was self-defeating. The rubble provided excellent defensive positions and the bomb craters hampered the deployment of armour. The fighting in the streets of Cassino resembled the ferocious battle of

Stalingrad, while on the slopes of Monte Cassino the Gurkhas fought hard for a few feet of ground. On 23 March Freyberg called off the attack. It had cost over two thousand men and had achieved none of its objectives.

General Alexander then shifted the British Eighth Army from the Adriatic to increase the pressure around Monte Cassino. A combined assault began on the night of 11 May. They broke through between Cassino and the coast. Monte Cassino eventually fell to the Polish Corps of the Eighth Army on 18 May.

A week later, the remaining German and Italian contingents of Army Group C – nearly a million men – surrendered to the Allied forces. The war in Italy at least was over

To defend the Gustav Line, Kesselring had had to take men away from Anzio, allowing the Allied forces there to break out. The Canadian Corps of the Eighth Army then took the Liri Valley and the Gustav Line began to collapse. General Mark Clark then made a dash for Rome. Assessing the situation, Kesselring declared Rome to be an 'open city' and evacuated his troops. Clark entered Rome on 5 June. It was a tremendous propaganda boost the day before D-Day. The capital of one of the enemy powers was now in Allied hands. However, militarily Clark's dash on Rome was a mistake. He had missed the chance to encircle the German troops withdrawing from the Gustav Line. Instead they had withdrawn in good order to another defensive line along the Arno River, 160 miles (260 km) north of Rome.

Nevertheless, on 7 June, Alexander reported to Churchill that not even the Alps could daunt his army. Churchill was thrilled at the prospect of the Allied armies taking Yugoslavia and even Vienna before the Russians got there. But even the British chiefs of staff doubted that Alexander could reach the Alps by the end of the year. They were right. Although the defensive line along the Arno was overrun on 13 August, the Germans withdrew to the heavily fortified Gothic Line further north.

The Allies spent another winter shivering high in the Apennines. However, their supply routes were kept open with the help of thousands of civilians, while the Germans suffered at the hands of partisans behind their lines. In the spring, the Allies' overwhelming air superiority came into play again.

The Dictator's Demise

On 25 April 1945, Allied armoured columns crossed the Po. A week later, the remaining German and Italian contingents of Army Group C – nearly a million men – surrendered to the Allied forces. The war in Italy at least was over. Mussolini was captured by partisans, trying to escape over the border into Switzerland disguised as a German soldier. On 28 April 1945, he and his mistress Claretta Petacci were shot and killed. Their bodies were hung upside down from lampposts in the Piazza Loreto in Milan.

Into Rome: General Mark Clark becomes the first Allied officer to enter the city of Rome, 5 June 1944. The move was widely regarded as a propaganda victory, but a military blunder

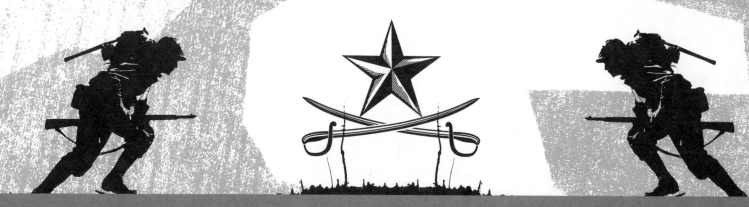

Chapter 7

THE LIBERATION OF FRANCE

DATES OF LIBERATION

6 JUNE-24 JULY

25 JULY-14 SEPT.

15 SEPT.- 15 DEC.

The liberation of Europe after D-Day: 6 June 1944

Since the Americans came into the war, the Soviet Union had been calling for landings in France, along with the opening of a second front. Churchill had been against it, particularly after a disastrous raid on Dieppe in August 1942, but his strategy to take the 'soft underbelly' of Europe through Italy seemed to be failing.

Early in the war, an attack on France had not been practical. Allied ships bringing men and material across the Atlantic were vulnerable to attack by German U-boats. However, by 1943, the German Enigma codes had been broken and advances in direction finding, sonar and depth charges had thwarted the U-boat menace. And Operation Overlord – the invasion of Normandy – was set for 5 June 1944.

Ready to Rumble

By the spring of that year some 2,000,000 tons of war materials had been assembled in Britain, including more than 50,000 tanks, armoured cars, jeeps and trucks. However, there were mishaps. Off the coast of Devon on 27 April 1944, German E boats slipped through offshore defences and killed 749 American servicemen practising for D-Day.

Meanwhile every effort was being made to deceive the Germans. While real tanks and armoured vehicles were hidden under trees, others made from rubber and plywood were left where German reconnaissance planes could spot them. Under Operation Fortitude, the fictitious First US Army Group under General Patton was assembled in southeast England, ostensibly bound for Calais.

American engineers inspect a captured German gun emplacement along the cliffs of Normandy. The emplacement was part of Hitler's 'Atlantic Wall' defensive line

Across the English Channel, the Atlantic Wall, a line of concrete fortifications and emplacements, stretched from Norway to Spain. However, when Field Marshal Erwin Rommel arrived in France to take charge, he found that many of the gun emplacements were half finished and fewer than half of the required mine fields had been laid. During the early months of 1944 Rommel began an energetic attempt to bring defences up to scratch.

D-Day

On 4 June the weather forecast was unseasonably bleak and, reluctantly, General Eisenhower, now supreme commander of the Allied Expeditionary Force, took a decision to postpone the invasion for twenty-four hours. Queasy troops already embarked were kept penned in the ships waiting for the gale to blow over.

The following day meteorologists forecast a clear spell and on 5 June 1944, over 1,200 fighting ships,

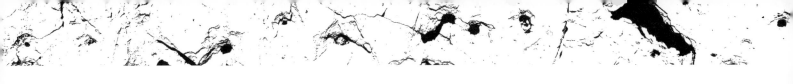

4,126 landing craft and 804 transport ships set sail from Britain. On board the Allied ships there were 132,000 young men destined for the beaches. The vast majority were repeatedly seasick.

As dawn rose on 6 June the Germans were confronted by this huge armada and the skies were full of Allied aircraft. By then some 23,500 British and American airborne troops had already been dropped inland. There was little organized resistance on the ground, the greatest danger coming from the swamps around the rivers Douve and Merderet, and the Dives valley that had been flooded by Rommel in preparation for the invasion. Some were killed in glider crashes and twenty parachutists came down in a village square, to be killed or taken prisoner by the Germans. Nevertheless, at dawn, men from the 82nd Airborne Division liberated St Mère Eglise, the first French village to be freed from German occupation.

This crucial bridge over the Caen Canal was captured in the early hours of D-Day by the British 6th Airborne Division, after whose winged horse insignia the bridge is now named

Pegasus Bridge

Men of the British 6th Airborne Division were tasked to capture the bridges that crossed the Caen Canal and the River Orne at Benouville. The first bridge controlled the access from the east, specifically the Pas de Calais. It has since been named Pegasus Bridge, for the division's winged horse insignia.

It was at this bridge that the invaders claimed their first German victim. A young sentry was cut down as he fired a flare to warn fellow soldiers. Moments later the first British casualty was felled by German machine gunners. His name was Lieutenant Herbert Denham Brotheridge and he had been hand picked to lead one of six thirty-man companies led into action that night by Major John Howard. Brotheridge's glider crash-landed into the barbed wire defences at about 2 am on 6 June and his men were first on to the bridge.

Other airborne troops were able to capitalize on the surprise element of the attack, wiping out small German posts. Then they hunkered down, waiting for the support of Allied troops from the beaches.

Even though the beaches' defences were being pounded by bombs, German commanders were unsure that D-Day had begun. They were not expecting the invasion in such poor weather conditions. The Allied air forces had also made diversionary attacks around Calais, again leading them to believe that the attack would come there. A fake armada, caused by Allied aircraft dropping metal foil, was seen on Germany radar screens, while dummy parachutists were dropped elsewhere.

The invasion force comprised ten Allied divisions, including three airborne, along with naval support. Awaiting them in Normandy were twenty-five static coastal divisions, sixteen infantry and parachute divisions and ten armoured and mechanical divisions, with seven divisions in reserve.

US LSTs land troops and tanks on Omaha Beach, scene of the most ferocious fighting of D-Day. Barrage balloons protect the ships from enemy air strikes

Atlantic Wall. There were also more underwater obstacles here than at other beaches. As the day progressed, the troops were pushed up the sands by the tide, leaving sappers unable to complete the task of clearing beach obstacles. Many died on the sands as the beach was swept with fire, while the pill boxes and gun emplacements were eventually knocked out by aircraft or naval guns.

By the afternoon, the defenders had been pushed back. Fresh soldiers had to fight in the dunes, swamps and countryside nearby. Company Sergeant-Major Stan Hollis of the Green Howards was awarded the Victoria Cross for single-handedly clearing a pill box and drawing enemy fire from two other men.

By the end of the day the casualties on Gold amounted to about a thousand.

Of the twenty-four thousand who attacked Juno Beach, fifteen thousand were Canadians while nine thousand were British. In common with other beaches the men of the first wave were thwarted by capsizing craft and enemy guns. The initial pounding by bombers had largely failed in its objective of making the thoroughfare safer.

Sword Beach was also reduced to chaos although once again men quickly made it to the exits. German defenders, at first surprised by the onslaught, soon recovered and mounted a stiff resistance.

It was at Sword Beach that Lord Lovat and his hand-picked Commandos – including German anti-fascists – disembarked with piper Bill Millin. Lovat walked through the water with the aid of a walking stick with his head held high. His aim was to boost morale – although the piper also served to draw enemy fire.

In the grey dawn, the American 1st and 4th Infantry Divisions were heading for beaches code-named 'Utah' and 'Omaha', while the British and Canadians were heading for 'Juno', 'Sword' and 'Gold' beaches. The five beaches were sited along a 55-mile (88-km) stretch of coast.

The British Beaches

On Gold, the invaders met organized resistance from the Germans and a solid section of the

The American Beaches

At Utah the landings were a textbook exercise. This was mainly because the airborne troops had knocked out German resistance. Out of 23,000 men landed on Utah Beach on 6 June there were only 197 killed or wounded.

It was a different story on neighbouring Omaha Beach where low cloud had prevented the bombers from mounting successful raids prior to the landings. Naval bombardment also fell short, leaving the German guns largely unscathed. However, the skippers of the supporting destroyers risked everything by bringing their vessels close to shore to provide as much cover as possible.

The defenders at Omaha were the battle-hardened men of the 352nd division who had recently returned from the Eastern Front. And the Allied amphibious tanks had been released far too early. Many had sunk, drowning their crews.

At low tide soldiers had several hundred yards to cover before finding shelter and fresh waves of men had to step over the bodies of fallen comrades before facing slaughter themselves. Many fell victim to machine-gun fire as the doors of the landing craft opened.

Soon the rising tide drowned the wounded and pushed other men up the beach into the line of fire. Supporting troops and machinery were kept at bay by beach defences. Units were split, radio communications non-existent, and escape routes

Soldiers of the 3rd Canadian Division ready themselves for the attack at Colombelle, Normandy

The British beach as further waves of troops are disembarked from LCIs – Landing Craft Infantry – to take their places in the front line

cluttered by wreckage. The blood bath continued for hours until an advance on the beach heights was begun about noon. Only during the afternoon did the American troops on Omaha succeed in silencing the German guns.

The final death toll on Omaha remains unclear, but it is thought that some 2,500 men died before D-Day was over. Perhaps three times that number were wounded. The US V Corps sustained two thousand casualties alone. Thereafter the landing was known as 'Bloody Omaha'.

By the close of D-Day about 155,000 Allied troops were ashore, but few of the targets set by the military planners had been achieved. However, the casualties were far less than some had feared, and Germany's hold on occupied Europe had been broken. Nevertheless, Hitler was jubilant, telling his

generals that the Allies were now within reach of the Wehrmacht, where they could be destroyed.

Into the Bocage

Although the Allies had established a bridgehead in Normandy, it was three weeks before US troops liberated the port of Cherbourg, and it was not until 18 July that British and Canadian troops captured Caen, just 7.5 miles (12 km) from the coast, which had been scheduled to fall on the first day.

Some men dug in when they should have advanced and intelligence regarding the whereabouts of German soldiers was poor. The area was covered with ancient hedgerows between six and 20 feet (1.8 and 6 m) in height growing atop earth banks, known as bocage. This gave the German defenders camouflaged firing positions and Allied tanks were

29 July 1944: US infantrymen advance at the double across machine-gunned ground towards enemy positions held by SS troops

rendered useless. However, the Allied troops could call up air support. The Germans were now chronically short of planes.

Aircraft pinned down German columns during daylight hours so convoys could only advance under cover of darkness.

Deeper into France, Allied bombing raids and sabotage by French resistance further disrupted the German supply network. Meanwhile, American troops from the Normandy beaches moved up the Cotentin Peninsula and besieged the port of Cherbourg.

Caen

Both the Germans and the Allies had identified Caen as the lynch pin of the battle for Normandy and 21st Panzer Division rushed to its defence. They were joined by the ultra-patriotic 12th SS-Panzer Division *Hitlerjugend*. Then when Montgomery's 7th Armoured Division ventured into Villers-Bocage, an important staging post en route to Caen, it was ambushed by 501st SS Heavy Tank Battalion, an elite unit equipped with the fearsome Tiger tank.

Rommel and von Rundstedt, when commander in the west, persuaded Hitler to visit France to assess the situation. On 17 June on the outskirts of Paris, Rommel explained that after the Allies took Caen they would break out towards Paris. He proposed regrouping the German divisions and attacking on the flanks.

Hitler was not interested. He believed that the V1 'doodlebug' flying bombs – the first had hit London four days earlier – and jet aircraft Germany had now developed would give them air supremacy. Rommel was refused his crucial troop movements and warned about 'defeatism', while von Rundstedt was replaced with the compliant Field Marshal Gunther von Kluge.

Indeed, the V1 – dubbed the doodlebug or buzzbomb in Britain – brought terror bombing back to London. About eight thousand V1s rained down on England until Allied troops overran the launch sites some three months after D-Day. They were followed by long-range V2 rockets carrying a one-ton warhead. They were only countered when 12,000-pound bombs, known as Tallboys, were deployed by the RAF to smash through the reinforced concrete bunkers where the V rockets were stored.

The development of the jet-powered Messerschmitt

Soldiers of an elite SS Division with their Panzer Mk VI Tiger E. The Tiger tank was the best tank on the Western Front, and posed a serious threat to British and American troops

Tilly-sur-Seulles, 19 June: engineers clear minefields after they have captured the town. A Bren carrier destroyed by mines lies in the foreground

Me262 was dealt a blow by Hitler himself, who demanded it had bomber as well as fighter capability. This delayed its mass production until the war was all but lost.

Mulberry Harbours

On 19 June the worst storm in forty years hit Normandy and wrecked the makeshift Mulberry harbours that had been towed across the Channel to land supplies. The Mulberry harbour on Omaha Beach, where 14,500 tons of cargo had been delivered, was damaged beyond repair. And it was not until 29 June that the Mulberry harbour at Arromanches was back in commission.

When the Americans finally took Cherbourg, they found the port facilities wrecked. However,

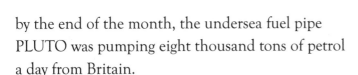

by the end of the month, the undersea fuel pipe PLUTO was pumping eight thousand tons of petrol a day from Britain.

Breaking Out to the East

On 26 June, Montgomery tried to push south and then east to take the high ground around Caen. Following some of the bitterest fighting yet seen, the 11th Armoured Division reached Hill 112, but were forced to retreat by three Panzer divisions.

On 4 July the Canadian 3rd Division, with support from the guns of warships, anchored off the coast and rocket-firing Typhoon fighters, tried to clear the western approaches to Caen but the tenacious 12th SS Panzer Division held fast during a two day onslaught.

On 7 July, some 2,300 tons of bombs were dropped on the northern sector of the city by 457 RAF planes, reducing it to ruins. This enabled the infantry to advance, but the bomb craters stopped tanks and armoured vehicles in their tracks. Deprived of protection soldiers picked their way through the smoking rubble under the fire of enemy snipers. After house-to-house fighting, the Germans withdrew to strong defensive positions across the River Orne, still able to harass Allied columns if they tried to push on.

Three days later the 43rd Wessex Division retook Hill 112 and held it for forty-eight hours before being beaten back by two Panzer divisions with the loss of two thousand casualties among the Wessex division alone. The hill changed hands several times. Rommel had said that he who holds Hill 112 controls Normandy.

Operation Goodwood began on 18 July with a massive aerial onslaught. Then troops and tanks eventually managed to clear the ruins of Caen.

They then advanced some 3 miles (5 km) towards Falaise where they were halted by German anti-tank guns poised on the Bourguebus Ridge. The operation was finally called off on 20 July. By then losses amounted to some four thousand men and five hundred tanks, more than a third of the total the British had in Normandy at the time.

By then, Rommel had been injured when his car was strafed by Allied planes on 17 July. Returning to Germany for convalescence, he was implicated in the 20 July bomb plot to kill Hitler and forced to commit suicide.

> *Rommel had been injured when his car was strafed by Allied planes. Returning to Germany for convalescence, he was implicated in the 20 July bomb plot to kill Hitler and forced to commit suicide*

The First Canadian Army led by General Henry Crerar came into Montgomery's operational sphere on 23 July while General George S. Patton brought his Third US Army into action on 1 August. As Rommel feared, once the British, American and Canadian armies gained a solid foothold on the Continent it would be doubly difficult to evict them.

The Falaise Gap

With Montgomery making slow progress in the east, Bradley, now commanding the US 12th Army Group, sent Patton and his Third Army on a long sweep south, then east, to encircle the Germans. Hitler saw the danger too late. He had ordered von

Kluge to switch four armoured divisions from the British front to attack the Americans, but Kluge could not disengage them until 7 August. Hitler planned a counterattack against the bottleneck at Avranches, closing the gap there and cutting off Patton's supply lines. Hitler, however, was 800 miles (1,300 km) away in his headquarters in East Prussia. His commanders on the ground in Normandy were against the attack. They knew that the battle of Normandy was lost, and that they should make an orderly retreat across the river Seine.

On the Run

Hitler threw in four divisions of the Fifteenth Army, fresh from the Pas de Calais. But Allied bombers cut off the German retreat by bombing the remaining bridges along the Seine. Meanwhile, Patton was making quick time across the open roads of northwest France, taking Le Mans on 8 August. To the north, on their way to Avranches, five Panzer and two infantry divisions ran into a single American division at Mortain, which managed to hold them until other Allied units came to its aid. Powerful US formations struck back through Vire, while the British pushed from the north against Condé and Patton turned north closing the trap. The Germans were now caught in a small pocket between Mortain and Falaise, where the Allied air forces relentlessly bombed and strafed them.

By 14 August, the only way out was through an 18-mile (30-km) gap between the Canadians at Falaise and Patton's Third Army. Patton wanted to drive on to Falaise and close the gap but, by then, his speeding army had lost its coherence and Bradley ordered

A shaken Hitler shows the visiting Mussolini his devastated bunker in the Wolf's Lair headquarters at Rastenburg in Prussia

him to stop. By this time, German units were being cut down by the French Resistance or surrendering wholesale to Allied forces. Kluge became lost in the confusion. Soon after he reappeared he was relieved of his command, and committed suicide. By 17 August, the Falaise gap was down to 11 miles (18 km) and the German forces were streaming east-wards through it. By 18 August, it was squeezed to 6 miles (10 km), and air attacks on it were so relent-

> 'The battlefield at Falaise was one of the greatest killing grounds of the war areas ... I was conducted through on foot to encounter a scene that could be described only by Dante'

less that any attempt to get through it resulted in almost certain death. It was sealed on 20 August.

Eisenhower said later of the battle: 'The battlefield at Falaise was unquestionably one of the greatest killing grounds of any of the war areas. Roads, highways and fields were so choked with destroyed equipment and with dead men and animals that passage through the area was extremely difficult. Forty-eight hours after the closing of the gap, I was conducted through on foot, to encounter a scene that could be described only by Dante. It was quite literally possible to walk for hundreds of yards at a time, stepping on nothing but dead and decaying flesh.'

Some ten thousand Germans were killed in six days in the Falaise Pocket, and fifty thousand prisoners were taken. Of the twenty thousand to fifty thousand who escaped, many more were killed before they reached the Seine. Thousands more who were cut off elsewhere gave themselves up. Two Panzer divisions and eight divisions of infantry were captured almost complete. In all, German casualties in Normandy amounted to 400,000 men, half of whom were captured. Allied casualties totalled 209,672 men, of whom 36,976 were killed. The Germans also lost 1,300 tanks, 1,500 guns and 20,000 vehicles.

By then, Allied forces also landed on the French Riviera in what became known as the 'champagne campaign'. The invaders were greeted on the beach by a Frenchman bearing a tray with a bottle of bubbly and glasses. 'Welcome, you are somewhat late,' the champagne bearer gently chided. Then Allied troops began mopping up in Vichy France. What remained of the German army in western Europe ran headlong for the German border.

The Liberation of Paris

By the middle of August, the Allies were so close to Paris that liberation would surely come in a matter of weeks. In fact the Parisians decided they could not wait that long. On hearing the boom of Allied gunfire on the city limits, the Resistance began an uprising in Paris on 19 August. With the Allies now at the gates of the city there could only be one outcome.

German commander General Dietrich von Choltitz was ordered by Hitler to burn Paris. It was to be reduced to a pile of rubble like Warsaw. Choltitz disobeyed and spared the city.

The Allies had been holding off liberating Paris for fear of civilian casualties. The decision was now reversed. An armoured division was sent forward. It arrived on the outskirts on 24 August. That evening General de Gaulle walked along the Champs Elysées regardless of the threat of German sniper fire. The following day, Paris's church bells rang out to mark the end of German occupation.

The mood was euphoric, but the mob then turned on collaborators. An investigation found that 4,167 summary executions of Frenchmen by Frenchmen took place after D-Day.

Two days prior to the liberation of Paris, Romania switched sides. King Michael I accepted Moscow's demands for an unconditional surrender while permitting German soldiers to leave without harassment. Bulgaria had already withdrawn from the Axis. But still Hitler refused to sue for peace.

Encouraged by the sound of Allied artillery around the city, the citizens of Paris take up arms against the German army of occupation

Chapter 8
THE MARCH ON GERMANY

After their defeat at Stalingrad, the Germans were on the retreat in Russia. But in the summer of 1943, they tried to seize the initiative once more. A huge salient 150 miles (240 km) wide had developed around Kursk with the Soviet lines protruding 100 miles (160 km) westwards into the German lines. On 15 April 1943 Hitler ordered Operation Zitadelle – 'Citadel' – to 'encircle the enemy forces situated in the region of Kursk and annihilate them by concentric attacks'. Guderian opposed this, fearing they would lose more tanks than they would be able to replace.

General Walther Model, commander of the German Ninth Army on the Eastern Front, was also against the operation. He produced air reconnaissance photographs that showed that the Russians had prepared strong defences there in anticipation of a German pincer movement and withdrawn most of their mobile force from the salient. But

Hitler ordered the assault to go ahead 'for political reasons'.

As the new Panther tanks were not ready until the end of May, the operation was put back until 15 June. By that time the Wehrmacht had assembled an assault force of fifty divisions – 900,000 men. These would be led by seventeen armoured divisions, with 2,700 tanks and mobile assault guns.

Soviet Defences

The Soviets knew what the Germans were planning and had plenty of time to organize defences between 16 and 25 miles (25 and 40 km) deep in the salient. Red Army engineers laid 400,000 mines in fields that would channel the German armoured units into nests of anti-tank guns. The Soviets had six thousand anti-tank guns, twenty thousand other artillery pieces, howitzers and mortars, and 920 rocket launchers. They outnumbered the Germans

Russian tanks and troops take on the SS *Totenkopf* Division, Kursk, 1943

in the field with seventy-five divisions and 3,600 tanks. In all, over two million men were involved, along with six thousand tanks and four thousand aircraft.

The German offensive was further delayed until 5 July, giving the Soviets more time to prepare their defences. Intelligence about the enemy's intentions allowed them to bombard the German assembly points twenty minutes before zero hour. The German Panzers were used to making lightning attacks, but by the evening of the first day they had advanced only 6 miles (10 km) through the Soviet defences.

> To the south things were no better. The Germans were outnumbered seven to one. Hitler refused to allow the troops there to withdraw to new defensive positions

The northern thrust of the pincer was halted on the second day just 12 miles (19 km) from the start line. The southern arm managed to penetrate 20 miles (32 km). Eight days into the battle, the Germans had taken 24,000 prisoners and destroyed or captured a hundred tanks and 108 anti-tank guns. Even so the gap between the two jaws of the pincers was still 75 miles (120 km).

On 12 July, a bitter engagement was fought near the village of Prokhorovka. The Red Army held. This was the turning point. The Soviets announced that the first phase of the battle was over and launched an offensive of their own against the Germans' Orel salient immediately to the north.

Hitler now faced a dilemma. He had already lost twenty thousand men. His offensive had stalled and he now had to withdraw some of his forces to defend Orel. Meanwhile British and American forces had landed on Sicily on 10 July, opening a second front. Troops would have to be sent to defend southern Italy. As a result he called a halt to Zitadelle.

Advantage Red Army

The Soviets now had the initiative. On 15 July, they began a counter-attack with an artillery barrage that, they boasted, was 'ten times heavier than at Verdun', the famous artillery barrage of World War I. The aim was to bombard the German minefields, blowing up as many mines as possible. Overhead there were huge air battles with heavy losses on both sides. Behind the German lines partisans began blowing up the railways to prevent supplies and reinforcements reaching the front. The Germans were forced to abandon the Orel salient, burning the crops behind them.

To the south things were no better. The Germans were outnumbered seven to one. And the Soviets kept bringing up reinforcements. Hitler refused to allow the troops there to withdraw to new defensive positions. On 30 July, a Panzer group had a limited success, forcing the Red Army back over the River Mius. But on 3 August the Soviets pounded the gap between German armies to the north and south of Kursk and sent a huge mechanized force through the breach. On 4 August, Orel had to be evacuated. The same day Belgorod to the south fell.

German Panzer groups roamed the battlefield, fighting sporadic actions. But nothing could halt the Soviet onslaught. While the Germans lost men as they pulled back, the Red Army gained conscripts with every mile they took. Within four days, they had advanced 70 miles (112 km) and Kharkov was in Russian hands on 23 August. The German army fought on for nearly another two years but, after Kursk, there was nothing they could do to prevent the Red Army driving forward all the way to Berlin.

Pulling Back

The Battle of Kursk marked the end of the German offensive capability on the Eastern Front. Huge numbers of men were lost, along with their equipment. It was now doubtful whether the Panzers had enough tanks to hold the Eastern Front, let alone take on the British and Americans if they landed, as anticipated, in the west.

The Germans had no alternative but to pull back. Hitler continued exhorting his commanders to counterattack and regularly gave orders they were to hold their position at all costs, resulting in massive losses. While the Germans were forced back the Soviets grew stronger. As the Russians prepared for their summer offensive of 1944, Stalin had at his disposal five hundred infantry and forty artillery divisions, three hundred armoured or mechanized brigades with nine thousand tanks and 16,600 aircraft.

A squad of Russian T-34 tanks opens fire at Kursk. The T-34 was revolutionary in design and featured sloped armour, a low silhouette and a heavy gun. Field Marshal von Kleist called it 'the finest tank of the war'

German commanders grew tired of Hitler's tactics that wasted lives unnecessarily. A plot was hatched to assassinate him. On 20 July 1944, Lieutenant Colonel Claus von Staffenberg left a bomb in a briefcase in the conference room at the Wolf's Lair, Hitler's field headquarters in Rastenberg, East Prussia. The bomb went off, but Hitler's life was saved by the massive oak support of the conference table. The conspirators were shot, forced to commit suicide or tortured to death.

Nothing could hold back the Soviet advance.

However, when the Russians reached Praga, a suburb on the Vistula opposite Warsaw on 31 July they halted. The Soviets then encouraged the underground in the city – the Home Army of around fifty thousand – to revolt. The Polish Home Army attacked the German garrison on 1 August and within three days had taken over most of the city. But the Germans sent reinforcements. For the next sixty-three days Warsaw was pounded by bombs and shells.

The Red Army did nothing and Stalin refused the western Allies permission to use Soviet airfields

I8 October 1944: German civilians board a US lorry in Aachen bound for a Belgian refugee camp to escape the battle for the city between German and American forces

to fly supplies into the beleaguered Poles. Without ammunition and food, the Home Army was forced to surrender on 2 October. Warsaw's population was deported and the city destroyed. When the Soviets finally forced the Germans out of Poland, the way was open for them to install their own pro-Soviet regime which remained in power until 1989.

The Low Countries

Having lost the battle for France, Germany now had to defend occupied territories in the Low Countries and Germany itself. The first German city to fall was Aachen, although its capitulation was a long, drawn-out affair. Troops from the First US Army approached the city on 12 September. However, defenders put up a staunch battle, often inspired by the sight of a corpse swinging from a tree – the punishment for those deemed insufficiently loyal to Hitler. It was not until 16 October that the city was surrounded by US soldiers and a further five days before its surrender. British and Canadian troops also faced unexpected losses as they mopped up along the Channel, where German troops had been ordered to fight to the last man, starving the Allies of fuel.

However, British commander Lieutenant-General Brian Horrocks had charged ahead into Belgium. Inspired by this, Montgomery planned an operation to secure a Rhine crossing at the Dutch town of Arnhem, along with four other vital river bridges. Starting out as a relatively small operation, this turned into the largest airborne assault in history – Operation Market Garden.

On 17 September paratroopers of the US 101st Airborne Division quickly secured bridges over the Wilhelmina and Zuiter Willemsvaart canals. The 82nd Airborne captured a bridge over the Meuse but failed to secure the one at Nijmegen in the face of a stout German counterattack.

A Bridge Too Far

At Arnhem, the remnants of two highly trained SS Panzer divisions, recently trained in techniques to repel airborne invasions, were, by happenstance, in the area for a re-fit. British paratroopers were dropped up to 8 miles (13 km) away to avoid flak, so lost the element of surprise. Besides, a copy of the attack plans was captured. Nevertheless, the paras captured the north end of one bridge at Arnhem and held it for six days.

Dunkirk veteran Lieutenant Ted Shaw and C Company were dropped at Arnhem to support the 3rd Battalion... He witnessed the Polish Parachute Brigade arriving in gliders

The British XXX Corps which was to relieve the paratroopers was held up by fierce German opposition. Polish paratroopers arriving five days after the initial attack were also kept away from the British at Arnhem by determined German fighters.

Dunkirk veteran Lieutenant Ted Shaw and C Company were dropped at Arnhem to support the 3rd Battalion with anti-tank guns. He witnessed the Polish Parachute Brigade arriving in gliders. They came under heavy fire that killed many before they touched the ground. He was asked to take on a German ack-ack gun that was causing havoc for the airborne troops, though he only had armour-piercing shells rather than high explosives that were

Men of the 1st Paratroop Battalion take cover in a shell hole during the battle for Arnhem, September 1944

needed for the job. He silenced the German gun, but at a price.

'Afterwards we took terrific casualties because the Germans knew where we were,' he said, and they lost all four guns.

He found himself in charge of 'walking wounded' in Oosterbeek after all the uninjured British soldiers had disappeared. He put up a white sheet at the basement where the injured men lay to indicate their surrender then tried to make his escape. He was wading across a stream when he was captured by an SS machine gunner.

'When he searched me he found Donald, a paratrooper duck made out of an old army blanket with a beret and medals,' said Shaw.

'Talisman?' his captor asked.

When Shaw said yes, he returned it.

'I also had ninety condoms on me, a pack of three for each of the thirty men in my troop,' said Shaw. 'He didn't give those back to me.'

The enemy was not always so amenable.

'One of the lads had his wallet taken and a picture of his wife torn up. When he made a move to protest he was shot where he stood,' recalled one

soldier from the 1st Parachute Brigade. 'Among the group was a teenage resistance worker who we had begged to get into army uniform in case he was caught but he stood there proudly wearing his orange armband. The German came up to him and said one word – terrorist – and shot this brave youngster through the head. His blood spilt all over me.'

Within nine days all the Allies at Arnhem were compelled to withdraw, leaving some 7,800 men either dead, wounded or prisoner. About 450 Dutch people also perished.

The Dutch in the immediate area were evicted and their belongings were looted. The Germans aimed to build a defensive line along the north river bank in case of future attacks. The wider Dutch population under occupation in northern Holland was kept short of food. In the 'Hunger Winter' an estimated 18,000 people died there before liberation came in April 1945.

Despite the failure of Operation Market Garden, the Allies continued to advance slowly in Belgium, taking the deep-water port of Antwerp on 26 November. It then came under attack by V1s and V2s.

Meanwhile, US troops reached the Siegfried Line that ran for 300 miles (480 km) from Basle to Cleves. But fuel shortages stalled the advance, giving the Germans valuable time to regroup.

Battle of the Bulge

Hitler ordered a counterattack in the thick of winter through the forested Ardennes, to split the Allied armies to the north and south. The man given the task was SS General Sepp Dietrich.

'All I had to do was cross the Meuse, capture Brussels then go on and take Antwerp,' Dietrich said later. 'All this through the Ardennes where

BATTLE OF THE BULGE: DECEMBER 1944–JANUARY 1945

.... Front line 16 December ____ Front line 20 December ——— Front line 25 December

The attempted breakthrough by massed Panzer armies in the Ardennes area of France was Hitler's last desperate gamble to stave off defeat by the Allies. It failed

snow was waist deep and there wasn't room for four tanks abreast, let alone six armoured divisions.'

Thirty divisions containing some half million troops were assembled, supported by some thousand aircraft primed to burst through American lines and split the Allied armies.

Allied commanders did not see the offensive coming. Reconnaissance flights were grounded due to bad weather and strict radio silence was maintained.

At first the German fightback seemed little more than an isolated pocket of resistance. However Eisenhower swiftly bolstered the thin US front line by halting other Allied activity in the region and diverting extra troops to the bulge in the line that gave the battle its name.

Two regiments of the 106th division of the First US Army were forced to surrender. However, the 101st Airborne troops at Bastogne held out. When asked by the surrounding Germans to surrender, commander Brigadier General Anthony McAuliffe replied in one word: 'Nuts!' Bastogne became the rock that split the German advance.

The Malmédy Massacre

Men from Battery B of the 285th Field Artillery Observation Battalion were cut down in cold blood on 17 December by an SS Panzer group from the elite *Leibstandarte Adolf Hitler* led by Colonel Joachim Peiper near Malmédy in Belgium. They had already surrendered and given up their weapons. Machine guns were turned on the unarmed Americans, then survivors were dispatched with a single shot by German soldiers strolling among the bodies.

Second Lieutenant Virgil Lary later testified: 'After the first machine guns fired men fell dead and wounded all around me... A man came by me as I lay feigning

American soldiers dig hasty foxholes in snow-covered terrain as enemy artillery fire opens up near Berismenil, Belgium. Ardennes campaign, December 1944

death and I heard a pistol shot nearby. Then I heard the sound of a new clip being inserted in a pistol and the individual passed me. I heard someone say to someone else: "Have they killed you yet?" He replied: "No, not yet ... but if the bastards are going to kill me I wish they would come back and get it over with." A bullet had severed my toes and I was in extreme pain and frozen from head to foot.

'Here and there I heard more raised voices: "Have they gone?" "What shall we do?" "Is it safe?" "Shall we make a run for it?"

'Suddenly about fifteen of us decided to make a break for it. We had moved a few yards when rifles cracked then a machine gun. I managed to clamber over a fence into a wood and ran along a dirt road until I came to a tumbledown shed. There were bundles of sticks inside and I pulled these all over myself. I waited.'

It was clear that the troops of the *Leibstandarte Adolf Hitler* were told to excel in the killing of prisoners-of-war as in fighting. After the war, Dietrich, Peiper and forty-two others were convicted of the massacre and sentenced to death. However, the sentences were commuted to life imprisonment and Peiper and Dietrich were released in 1958.

Today a memorial with the names of the eighty-four dead stands at the crossroads at Malmédy.

Battling the Weather

The Allied cause during the Battle of the Bulge was hampered by bad weather that kept fighters grounded. Only when the skies cleared on 22 December did the balance of the battle change. The following day

The bodies of murdered American prisoners-of-war lie where they have fallen in the snowy fields around Malmédy. The massacre was perpetrated by the elite SS *Leibstandarte Adolf Hitler* Division

Allied aircraft attacked thirty-one different targets, inhibiting the movement of the Panzers and disrupting supply lines.

On 27 December a last-ditch effort to deprive the Allies of air superiority with the Luftwaffe bombing twenty-seven different airfields foundered. But while 156 Allied aircraft were destroyed, a further three hundred Luftwaffe planes were shot down.

The advance was halted by a shortage of petrol and, by the middle of January, the battle was over. Hitler's last ditch effort in the Ardennes had failed. Before that, on 18 October 1944 Hitler had established a new fighting force, the *Volkssturm*. It was open to all available men aged between sixteen and sixty, though later boys as young as ten were asked to arm themselves. Hitler made it clear that it was everyone's duty to fight – to the death, if necessary.

The Bombing Campaign

While two great armies marched on Germany from the east and west, the country was being laid waste by a bombing campaign. Britain's Air Chief Marshal Sir Arthur Harris, commander in chief of British Bomber Command, believed that obliterating German cities would lead to a collapse in the national will to wage war. Meanwhile his American counterpart General Carl 'Tooey' Spaatz thought that knocking oil installations out was the key to winning victory. Both pursued their agendas.

The full-scale bombing of Germany began in September 1944 when Eisenhower relinquished first claim on all available aircraft for the purposes of tactical air support during the Normandy campaign. In the next seven months more than 800,000 tons of bombs fell on Germany and thousand-bomber raids became commonplace.

One of Germany's last remaining precious Panzers, knocked out by American artillery during the German counter-attack in the Ardennes

One of the prime targets for the Allies was the Leuna chemical fuel works 100 miles (160 km) south of Berlin. It was bombed on twenty-two different occasions, reducing its output to on average just 9 per cent of its capacity. Fears that the German war machine would be brought to a complete standstill from lack of fuel were looming large. Railway depots, transport yards, factories and industrial heartlands were relentlessly pounded.

Luftwaffe commander General Adolf Galland planned one final operation against the Allies to reduce their ability to bomb fuel depots. He knew it would cost the Luftwaffe dear but felt the losses would be worthwhile if the capabilities of the enemy airpower were likewise impaired.

On New Year's Day 1945, in concert with Hitler's Ardennes offensive, some nine hundred Messerschmitts and Focke-Wulfs attacked Allied air bases on the continent, destroying some 206 Allied aircraft. But the Allies made a swift recovery. As they pursued the Luftwaffe back to Germany, some 253 Luftwaffe pilots were killed, wounded or taken prisoner. It was a blow from which the Luftwaffe would not recover. Harris and Spaatz could now continue unopposed.

The Bombing of Dresden

A bombing raid against Dresden took place on 13 and 14 February 1945. Choked with refugees, the Germans were convinced that 'Florence on the Elbe' would never be bombed. There were no reinforced bomb shelters, except those built by the city burghers. The guns that could have defended the city had been moved to the Ruhr.

The first wave of 234 RAF Lancaster bombers hit the city for seventeen minutes under cover of darkness. Three hours later, 538 RAF planes arrived, targeting the perimeter of the area already destroyed. In daylight the American Flying Fortresses came, nominally aiming for the city's railway stations and marshalling yards. The result was firestorms of the kind already experienced in Hamburg. In essence, the numerous fires combined to create one massive ball of flames so the city was turned into an inferno.

Lothar Metzger was nine years old when the attack happened and sought shelter from the bombs with his mother and four sisters.

'The broken remains of our house were burning,' he said. 'On the streets there were burning vehicles and carts with refugees, people, horses, all of them screaming and shouting in fear of death... We saw terrible things: cremated adults shrunk to the size of small children, pieces of arms and legs, dead people, whole families burnt to death, burning people ran to and fro, burnt coaches filled with civilian refugees, dead rescuers and soldiers, many were calling and looking for their children and families, and fire everywhere, everywhere fire, and all the time the hot wind of the firestorm threw people back into the burning houses they were trying to escape from.'

Ultimately, attempts to identify and bury the dead proved futile and mass cremations were organized. No one knows the death toll, but it seems likely that at least 25,000 died.

Allied bombing of Germany only slowed after the start of April when victory was assured. There was no merit now in wiping out industrial centres and communications networks that would be needed by occupying troops.

Miraculously undamaged, statues peer down in disbelief at the destruction of the city of Dresden in the aftermath of the Allied bombing

Chapter 9

INTO THE REICH

US soldiers cross the Rhine river: troops of the 9th Armored Division, First US Army, move forward over the bridge at Remagen, Germany to establish a bridgehead in strength on the east bank

On 7 March a detachment of Americans from the 9th Armored Division, part of the First Army, emerged from the Eifel Woods on the west bank of the Rhine to find the Ludendorf railway bridge, near Remagen, intact. Every other bridge along the river had been destroyed by retreating Germans on the orders of Hitler.

Lieutenant Karl Timmermann led his men towards the bridge to be greeted by the roar of explosives. But somehow the bridge was left standing. Within twenty-four hours some eight thousand troops, along with tanks and self-propelled guns, made use of it.

After five divisions were across, on 17 March, the bridge collapsed, killing twenty-six. By then the Americans had built several pontoon bridges. Seven Wehrmacht officers who had left the bridge standing were executed, while V2 rockets turned on the bridgehead. Hitler then instituted a scorched earth policy inside Germany, believing that a nation that could not give him victory did not deserve to survive.

On 22 March Patton's forces made amphibious crossings of the Rhine at Oppenheim, between Mainz and Mannheim. The following day Montgomery parachuted men across the Rhine out of two thousand aircraft. Five days after establishing bridgeheads the respective armies broke out into Germany.

Inside the Nazi Camps

On 28 March Eisenhower directed his men towards Leipzig, leaving the Russians to take Berlin. But with no sign of surrender, the numerically superior Allies came to the conclusion they would have to fight through every inch of Germany to secure its defeat.

The liberation of concentration camps cast Hitler, his army and his people in a new light. Dr Robert Hartley Olver who was with R Deception Force was one of the first into Bergen-Belsen concentration camp after it had been liberated and immediately packed a first aid bag and set out to see if he could help.

Soldiers of the US 6th Armored Division dodge sniper fire during the capture of Oberdola, Germany

'We smelled the stench a mile away and soon found ourselves taking part in the most horrible experience of our lives,' he said. 'The high barbed wire gates were open and just outside we saw a few dozen victims on their stomachs eating the grass and weeds that had survived outside the camp – our first sight of those dreadful striped pyjamas covering virtual skeletons. The main wide road through the camp was thickly strewn with the dead and dying. If the skeleton moved it was still alive. Amongst them were males and females squatting with uncontrollable diarrhoea.

'One of the largest wooden huts lining the main road was the so-called hospital. The dead and dying were so piled up inside that they blocked the windows and jammed the one door. To me the over-riding horror was the fact that the vast proportion of inmates were so far gone that they did not appreciate the fact they were being rescued. To them, one uniform was the same as another.

'As this was the first morning – organized help was just starting – in one area the brutal male guards and foul women in their belts and jackboots were being compelled at bayonet point to collect the dead and carry them to the mass graves. I heard later that some were pushed into the grave to get out as best they could.

'Just inside the gates was an immense neat pile about five feet high and the same wide, stretching for yards composed entirely of boots, shoes and sandals, ripped

The Beast of Belsen: commandant of the camp at Bergen-Belsen, Josef Kramer, under British guard

The Stench of Death

It is estimated the British found ten thousand unburied bodies, mass graves containing a further forty thousand bodies and 38,500 people barely alive. Of these, about 28,000 died soon afterwards despite the efforts of the medics.

At Belsen and other concentration camps, local people were forced to visit and witness the abject cruelty that had gone on in their name. Pacifist Ron Tansley with the Friends Ambulance Unit was charged with clearing the Neuengamme concentration camp and found a local priest to recruit a hundred helpers from among the townspeople.

'I told him: "I'm surprised that you, a man of God, could allow the events at the camp to happen." He turned up his sleeve and there was a concentration camp number tattooed on his arm. He had spoken out against it and a few days later he was inside the gates himself. Then he turned to me and asked: "What would you have done?" I have often thought about that since.'

Prisoners of war usually received better treatment. Lieutenant Shaw, captured at Arnhem, found he had more to fear from the RAF than his captors. He was transported from Holland in cattle trucks. When RAF planes came over the German guards would dive off the train to leave the prisoners at the mercy of Allied fire.

He finally arrived at Oflag 79, an officers' camp

from the victims and awaiting transport to recycling plants. Most of the females had shaved heads and I found out much later that it all went to be woven into soft shoes for the U-boat crews.

'The excuse given by the odd officer was that the starvation was due to our own forces destroying all communicating roads and rails. They did not realize that we had entered a large new SS training establishment about half a mile away which was filled to bursting with food and medical supplies of all description and also a large fully appointed hospital complete with its staff of doctors and nurses.

'My most poignant memory was to see two little girls aged about four or five, dressed in shabby frocks which were quite clean. Their parents must have sacrificed all for them as they were reasonably nourished. These two were walking along the main road hand in hand, chatting to each other and neatly stepping over limbs and bodies as if they were just having a walk through a stony field.'

in Brunswick, on 20 October. There he was one of 2,430 in the camp from fifteen different countries. In a notebook he recorded the daily rations. Breakfast was Ersatz coffee – made from acorns – while for lunch there were three boiled potatoes plus hot water. In the afternoon there was Ersatz tea (without milk) to be followed by soup, made of turnips, barley or other equally humble ingredients. In six months, he lost 14 pounds (6.4 kg).

He did not recall any cruel treatment from the guards, although the execution of fifty escapees from Stalag Luft III occurred just six months earlier. On 12 April 1945 the prisoners at Oflag 79 awoke to find their guards missing and liberating American forces at the gate.

The Allied advance continued, challenged but largely unchecked. On 1 April Model's Army Group was enveloped in the Ruhr and thousands were taken prisoner, while Model committed suicide in a wood near Duisburg. Nevertheless, the Wehrmacht continued its doomed resistance.

From the Vistula to Berlin

The Soviets made their first attempt to invade East Prussia on 16 October 1944. Forty divisions backed by aircraft and armour covered a front of just 90 miles (144 km). They faced the fifteen divisions of the German Fourth Army which was stretched out over 220 miles (354 km). While trying to cross the River Angerapp, the Russians were thrown back, leaving evidence of atrocities. Nazi propaganda minister Joseph Goebbels made great play of this. As a result, some three months later six million Germans fled before the Russian invasion in temperatures of twenty degrees below zero.

During the Battle of the Bulge, Guderian was ordered to stabilize the Eastern Front. He pulled all

the Panzer and Panzergrenadier divisions out of the line to form a mobile reserve. But twelve under-strength divisions was not an adequate reserve to hold a front 725 miles (1,166 km) long. So Guderian planned to establish a large and well-camouflaged line of defence 12 miles (19 km) behind the line.

Hitler refused to accept the loss of 12 miles

Advancing Russian troops charge down a Polish street, during the push to the Elbe, 1944

without a fight and ordered that the second line be prepared just one or two miles behind the front. When the great Russian tidal wave came, it simply swamped both the defensive lines and the reserves. Hitler then claimed that he had always favoured a twelve-mile gap.

'Who was the half-wit who gave such idiotic orders?' he asked.

Guderian pointed out that it was he himself who had made the decision. Hitler called for the minutes of the autumn planning meetings to be brought. But he broke off reading them after a couple of sentences.

Hitler continued to insist that he was the military genius who had been commanding the Wehrmacht for five years. But nothing could stop the Russians. By 5 December they had reached the outskirts of Budapest and by Christmas Eve they had encircled the city.

When it became clear that the Ardennes offensive was a failure, Guderian begged for the attack to be called off and the remaining forces to be switched to the Eastern Front. He pointed out that the production from the factories in the Ruhr had been halted by enemy bombing. If they lost the industrial area of Upper Silesia to the Russians, they would no longer have the weapons-making capacity. But his request was denied. Indeed, Hitler ordered a further weakening of the Polish Front by ordering General Reinhardt's reserves to go to Budapest to lift the siege.

Cold Comfort

On New Year's Eve, Guderian went to Hitler's headquarters to ask for reinforcements in the east once again. But three divisions on the Western Front and one in Italy that were ready to be transported to the east were sent to Hungary instead of Poland.

On 12 January 1945, huge numbers of men and tanks began pouring over the Vistula into the Russian bridgeheads. Over the next few days, the Russians went on the offensive down the entire line and the front began to disintegrate.

On 16 January, Hitler returned to the partly bombed Chancellery in Berlin. He now decided that the Western Front should go on the defensive to release troops to fight in the east. But the Red Army was advancing rapidly across Poland and the Nazi extermination camp of Auschwitz-Birkenau had to be abandoned.

Established in April 1940, it became the biggest of the death camps and it is thought that between a million and 2.5 million people died there, most of them deliberately gassed. On 17 January 1945, inmates were transported to other concentration camps including Dachau and Mauthausen. Towards the end of the war, as Allied forces advanced through Europe, the Nazis hurriedly closed many of the camps to remove evidence of their crimes. Vast numbers of malnourished prisoners were forced to walk hundreds of kilometres to camps inside German territory. Thousands died on these 'death marches' and, when the Red Army arrived at Auschwitz on 27 January, there were 7,650 inmates left in the camp.

Strategic Retreat

Rather than risk being encircled, the German garrison in Warsaw withdrew, leaving the Red Army to continue its dash for the German border unhindered. Hitler was furious and gave orders for several staff officers to be arrested. Guderian took the blame and was then forced to submit to lengthy interrogations when he should have been concentrating all his efforts on the battle for the Eastern Front.

On 18 January, the Germans in Hungary attacked in an attempt to lift the siege of Budapest. They fought their way through to the banks of the Danube. But that same day the Russians entered the city, so the effort had been wasted. Nevertheless Hitler sent the Sixth Panzer Army to Hungary in an attempt to hold the Russians there.

On 20 January, the Russians set foot on German soil. The onslaught could not be resisted and Hitler began to accuse his Panzer commanders

Auschwitz-Birkenau was the biggest of the Nazi death camps and it is thought that between a million and 2.5 million people died there, most of them deliberately gassed

of treason. But the Red Army had now mastered the art of Panzer warfare. Advancing rapidly, they bypassed strong points and outflanked fortified lines. Guderian proposed that they open negotiations for an armistice on the Western Front as the Russians would be at the gates of Berlin in three or four weeks. When Hitler heard of this, Guderian was also accused of treason.

Breathing Space

Guderian then proposed a plan that would give them some breathing space. They should form a new Army Group specifically to hold the centre of the line. Guderian suggested its commanding officer should be Field Marshal Freiherr von Weichs, a commander in the Balkans. Hitler approved Guderian's plan for the creation of a new Army Group, but gave its command to Himmler. Guderian was appalled. Himmler was not a military man. He was a politician, the head of the SS and architect of the Final Solution to exterminate Europe's Jews. He was also Chief of Police, Minister of the Interior and Commander in Chief of the Training Army. Any one of these positions was a full-time job. But Hitler was insistent. Guderian tried to persuade him at least to give Himmler von Weichs' experienced staff. But Hitler, who was now wary of all his generals, allowed Himmler to choose his own staff. Himmler surrounded himself with other SS leaders who were largely, in Guderian's opinion, incapable of doing the jobs they had been given.

T-34s pick up infantrymen as they advance down the main highway from Seelow to Berlin

Some of the 7,650 survivors of Auschwitz discovered by the Russians when they liberated the camp on 27 January 1945

SS Brigade Leader Lammerding was Himmler's chief of staff. Previously the commander of a Panzer division, Lammerding had no idea of the duties of a staff officer. Adding to the air of unreality, the new Army Group was to be called Army Group Vistula, though the Russians had crossed the Vistula months before.

Hitler set up new 'tank destroyer' divisions. These consisted of men issued with anti-tank grenades and bicycles. Somehow they were expected to stop the huge armies of T-34s that were now driving westwards. By this time sixteen-year-old boys were being conscripted into the army.

The War is Lost

By 28 January, Upper Silesia was in Russian hands. Armaments Minister Albert Speer wrote to Hitler saying: 'The war is lost.' Hitler now cut Speer completely and refused to see anyone alone in private, because they always told him something he did not want to hear. He began demoting officers on a whim and brave soldiers denounced by party members found themselves in concentration camps without even the most summary investigation. Guderian found that more and more of his day was spent listening to lengthy monologues by Hitler as he tried to find someone to blame for the deteriorating

Members of the German *Volkssturm* on parade, many of whom were equipped with a *Panzerfaust* (a one-shot, anti-tank weapon), and sent out on bicycles to destroy Russian tanks

military situation. Hitler often became so enraged that the veins on his forehead stood out, his eyes bulged and members of staff feared that he might have a heart attack.

On 30 January, the Russians attacked the Second Panzer Army in Hungary and broke through. Guderian proposed evacuating the Balkans, Norway and what remained of Prussia and bringing back all the Panzers into Germany for one last battle. Instead Hitler ordered an attack. On 15 February the Third Panzer Army under General Rauss went on the offensive. In overall command of the offensive was General Walther Wenck. But on the night of the 17th, after a long briefing by Hitler, Wenck noticed that his driver was tired and

took the wheel himself. Wenck then fell asleep and crashed into the parapet of a bridge on the Berlin-Stettin highway. He was badly injured and, with Wenck in hospital, the offensive bogged down and never regained its momentum.

In March, Rauss was summoned to the Chancellery and asked to explain himself. Hitler did not give him a chance to speak. After he had dismissed Rauss, Hitler insisted he be relieved of his command. Guderian protested that he was one of the most able Panzer commanders. Hitler said that he could not be trusted because he was a Berliner or an East Prussian.

It was then pointed out that Rauss was an Austrian, like Hitler himself. Even so, he was relieved of his

post and replaced by General Hasso von Manteuffel.

Demotion for Himmler

Himmler's Army Group Vistula did little to halt the Russian advance and Guderian eventually suggested that Himmler be replaced. On 20 March, Hitler agreed. He was replaced by a veteran military man, Colonel-General Gotthard Heinrici, who was currently commanding the First Panzer Army in the Carpathians. At his disposal was the Third Panzer Army under General von Manteuffel, which occupied the northern part of the front. The centre was held by General Theodor Busse's Ninth Army, while the south was held by the depleted Army Group of Field Marshal Ferdinand Schörner. And there were thirty other divisions in the vicinity of Berlin he could call on.

Guderian continued to come up with suggestions of how the Russians' advance could at least be slowed. But after one final falling out with Hitler, he was ordered to take six weeks' convalescent leave for the sake of his health. He left Berlin on 28 March and intended to go to a hunting lodge near Oberhof in the Thuringian Mountains, but the rapid advance of the Americans made this impossible. Instead he decided to go to the Ehenhausen sanatorium near Munich for treatment of his heart condition. Warned that he might invite the attentions of the Gestapo, Guderian arranged to be guarded by two members of the Field Police.

Although Stalin had told Eisenhower that he intended to attack Berlin in May, his generals Zhukov and Ivan Konev were clear that he wanted to do it before that, even though their armies were exhausted after weeks of heavy fighting. Konev's 1st Ukranian Front – or Army Group – was on the eastern bank of the River Neisse, some 75 miles

(120 km) south-east of Berlin. He proposed starting his offensive with a two-and-a-half hour artillery bombardment with 7,500 guns. At dawn, he would lay smoke and force a river crossing with two tank and five field armies, over 500,000 men in all. He would keep his tanks on his right flank. They would smash through the German defences, then swing north-westwards and make a dash on Berlin. Unfortunately his plan relied on two extra armies that had been promised, which could not be relied on to arrive in time.

Zhukov's 1st Belorussian Front was on the Oder river, 50 miles (80 km) east of Berlin, with a bridgehead on the western side of the river at Küstrin. He proposed a pre-dawn bombardment with ten

> *Zhukov proposed a pre-dawn bombardment with ten thousand guns. Then he would turn 140 anti-aircraft searchlights on the German defenders, blinding them while he attacked*

thousand guns. Then he would turn 140 anti-aircraft searchlights on the German defenders, blinding them while he attacked. Two tank armies and four field armies would stream out of the Küstrin bridgehead, with two more armies on each flank. With complete air superiority and 750,000 men at his disposal, Zhukov was confident of a quick victory.

Green Light

Stalin gave Zhukov the green light as he was closer to Berlin and was better prepared. But, still encouraging the rivalry between the two field marshals, he also let Konev know that he was free to make a dash on Berlin if he thought he could beat Zhukov to it. The starting date set for the offensive was 16 April. The two field marshals had just thirteen days to prepare.

On 15 April, the Americans entered the race when Lieutenant-General William Simpson's Ninth Army crossed the Elbe. Between him and Berlin stood the remnants of the German Twelfth Army under General Wenck. There would be little that it could do to prevent Simpson making a dash for the capital. But Eisenhower ordered Simpson to halt on the Elbe until the link-up with the Red Army had been made at Dresden. The following morning at 0400, three red flares lit up the skies over the Küstrin bridgehead. It was followed by the biggest artillery barrage ever mounted on the eastern front. Mortars, tanks, self-propelled guns, light and heavy artillery – along with four hundred Katyushas – all pounded the German positions. Entire villages were blasted into rubble. Trees, steel girders and blocks of concrete were hurled into the air. Forests caught on fire. Men were deafened by the guns and shook uncontrollably. They were blinded by the searchlights. Then, after thirty-five minutes of pounding, the Soviets attacked.

Bunker Mentality

In his fortified bunker under the Reichschancellery, Hitler still believed that he could win the war. He predicted the Russians would suffer their greatest defeat at the gates of Berlin. His maps told him so. They were still covered in little flags representing SS and Army units. Unfortunately, most of these little flags were just... little flags. The units they represented had long since ceased to exist or were so chronically under strength that they were next to useless. Anyone who pointed this out was dismissed.

Heinrici was now in charge of the defence of the city. He was an expert in defensive warfare. On the eve of the Soviet attack, he had pulled his front-line troops back so that Zhukov's massive bombardment fell on empty positions. The Ninth Army had dug in on the Seelow heights, blocking the main Küstrin-Berlin road. Zhukov's men attacking down the road suffered terrible casualties.

They eventually overwhelmed the Seelow line with sheer weight of numbers, but then they came up against more German defences, reinforced by General Karl Weidling's 56th Panzerkorps, and were halted. Stalin was furious. He ordered Konev, who was making good progress to the south, to turn his forces on Berlin. And on 20 April, Marshal Konstantin Rokossovsky's 2nd Belorussian Front made a separate attack on von Manteuffel's Third Panzer Army.

Busse's Ninth Army began to disintegrate and Zhukov got close enough to Berlin to start bombarding the city with long-range artillery. Konev's forces were also approaching from the south and the German capital was caught in a pincer movement. To ensure that the Americans would not come and snatch their prize at the last moment, both Zhukov and Konev sent forces on to meet up with Simpson on the Elbe. They made contact at Torgau on 25 April to find Simpson sitting on the Elbe, facing no one. Two days earlier, Wenck had been ordered back for the defence of Berlin. On 28 April, he had reached the suburb of Potsdam. There he met fierce Soviet resistance. But he managed to extricate his force and tried to link up with remnants of the Ninth Army. Then he went westwards in the hope of surrendering to the Americans. Hitler cursed his treachery.

Desperate Measures

What propaganda minister Joseph Goebbels now

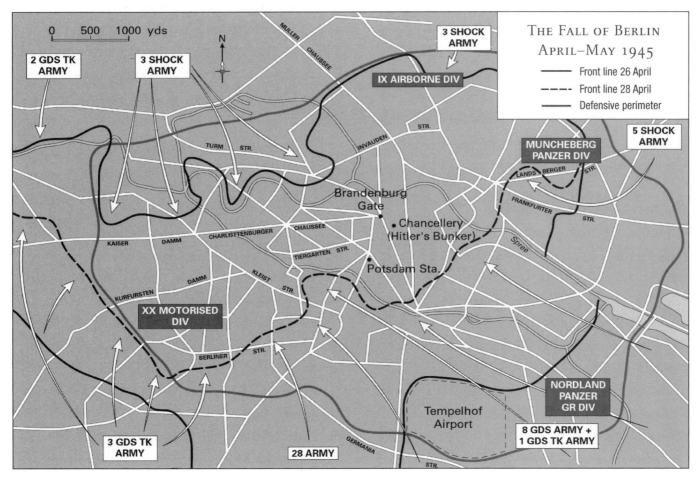

The map shows troop positions with labels: 2 GDS TK ARMY, 3 SHOCK ARMY, 3 SHOCK ARMY, IX AIRBORNE DIV, 5 SHOCK ARMY, MUNCHEBERG PANZER DIV, XX MOTORISED DIV, 3 GDS TK ARMY, 28 ARMY, NORDLAND PANZER GR DIV, 8 GDS ARMY + 1 GDS TK ARMY. Street and landmark labels: MULLER CHAUSSEE, TURM STR., INVAUDEN, STR., LANDS BERGER, FRANKFURTER, STR., Brandenburg Gate, Chancellery (Hitler's Bunker), Spree, KAISER DAMM, CHARLOTTENBURGER CHAUSSEE, TIERGARTEN STR., Potsdam Sta., KURFURSTEN DAMM, KLEIST STR., BERLINER STR., GERMANIA STR., Tempelhof Airport.

Legend: THE FALL OF BERLIN APRIL–MAY 1945 — Front line 26 April / Front line 28 April / Defensive perimeter. Scale: 0 500 1000 yds. N (compass).

Russian forces had 'Fortress Berlin' surrounded and it was only a matter of time before the Germans were pounded into submission

called 'Fortress Berlin' was defended by ninety-thousand ill-equipped boys from the Hitler Youth and elderly men from the *Volkssturm*. The two million Berliners still trying to go about their business in the ruined city joked: 'It will take the Russians exactly two hours and fifteen minutes to capture Berlin – two hours laughing their heads off and fifteen minutes to break down the barricades.'

To the end Hitler maintained that a relief column of Tiger IIs was on its way and loyal follower SS Obersturmführer Babick, battle commandant of the Reichstag, was at his map day and night planning for the arrival of these King Tigers.

'Babick was still bubbling over with confidence,' said Gerhard Zilch, an NCO with the 3rd Heavy Flak Battery. 'He thought he was safe in his shelter. SS sentries were posted outside. Others guarded the corridors of the Reichstag and the King Tigers, our finest weapon, were apparently just around the corner. He had divided his men into groups of five to ten. One group was commanded by SS-Untersturmführer Undermann – or something like that, I did not quite catch his name. He was posted to Ministry of the Interior – "Himmler's House" – south of the Molke bridge, with the bridge itself in his line of fire. Then an SS subaltern, about nineteen years old, came to Babick and reported that Undermann and his men had come across some alcohol and that they had got roaring drunk. He had brought Undermann with him and he was waiting outside. Babick roared: "Have him shot on the spot." The subaltern clicked his heels and marched out. Moments later, there was a burst of machine-gun fire. The boy returned and reported that the order had been carried out. Babick put him in charge of Undermann's unit.'

The Rats Leave the Sinking Ship

Himmler, Göring and other top Nazis left the city. Hitler refused to go, pretending, for a while, that the situation could be reversed. He issued a barrage of orders to his non-existent armies. Then, as the Soviets drew the noose tighter and fifteen thousand Russians guns pounded the city, Hitler dropped all pretence of running things and announced that he would commit suicide before the Russians arrived. Meanwhile the forty or fifty people left in the cellar of the Reichstag began looking for places to hide.

As Soviet troops entered the city, Hitler sacked Göring as his designated successor, for trying to take over while he was still alive, and Himmler, for trying to put out peace feelers to the British and Americans. Grand Admiral Karl Dönitz was named as Hitler's new successor.

Even though the situation was now hopeless, fanatical Nazis continued their resistance with hand-to-hand fighting. While a corps of Konev's tank troops entered the city from the south and Zhukov's Second Guards Tank Army entered from the north, taking Charlottenburg, detachments of the Hitler Youth held the Pichelsdorf bridge over the Havel and the bridge to Spandau. Elsewhere the last few Tiger tanks of the SS 'Hermann von Salza' battalion took on the Third Shock Army and the Eighth Guards Army in the Tiergarten.

Final Days of the Doomed Regime

Then news came that Mussolini was dead. The following day, 29 April, Hitler married his mistress Eva Braun. The next day, he dictated his will and his final political testament. That afternoon, in their private quarters, Hitler and his wife of one day committed suicide. Their bodies were burnt in a shallow trench in the Chancellery Gardens.

Both Zhukov's and Konev's troops were now in the city. But Konev was ordered to halt so that Zhukov's men would have the honour of raising the Red Flag on the Reichstag. Zhukov's resulting popularity was later seen as a threat by Stalin who banished him to obscurity in 1946.

There were still pockets of resistance and those remaining in Hitler's bunker tried to negotiate surrender terms. The Soviets would accept nothing but unconditional surrender and unleashed a new hurricane of fire. Goebbels and his wife killed their six children, then committed suicide. Hitler's closest adviser Martin Bormann tried to escape and he was thought to have been killed. If so, he was the only one of the top Nazis to have died in the fighting. The rest committed suicide. There were persistent rumours in the 1960s that Bormann had escaped to South America and was living in Paraguay. However, forensic experts established 'with near certainty' that one of two bodies unearthed during construction work in Berlin in 1972 was his.

The Red Flag Flies High

General Weidling eventually agreed to unconditional surrender in Berlin on 2 May. Later that day, the Reichstag was taken. Soviet reports say that a howitzer was rolled into Wilhelmplatz to blow off the doors and hand-to-hand fighting continued inside, though this seems unlikely. Major Anna

Nikulina from the political department of the 9th Rifle Corps of the Fifth Shock Army placed a red banner on the roof.

The surrender of the German forces in north-western Europe was signed at Montgomery's headquarters on Lüneburg Heath on 4 May. Another surrender document, covering all the German forces, was signed with more ceremony at Eisenhower's headquarters at Reims. And at 0028 on 8 May 1945, the war in Europe was officially over.

That day, Eisenhower's deputy Air Chief Marshal Sir Arthur Tedder and General Spaatz of the USAAF flew to Berlin to witness the signing of another surrender document at the head-quarters of the 1st Belorussian Front in front of Marshal Zhukov. Most of the fighting ended that day, but due to difficulties in communica-tion some resistance continued until 10 May.

While the various signings of the surrender were going on, hundreds of thousands of Wehrmacht soldiers managed to get past Bradley and Montgomery's advanced guards and surrender to the Western Allies and the Kriegsmarine used its last hours of freedom to evacuate as many troops as possible from the Baltic. Colonel-General C. Hilpert, now in charge of the beleaguered soldiers of what was now known as Army Group Kurland, surrendered just under 200,000 men to the Russians – all that was left of his two armies, five corps or sixteen divisions – and General Noak surrendered the three divisions of XX Corps on the Hela peninsula at the mouth of the Vistula. The fourteen divisions of the German Twentieth Army occupying Norway – 400,000 Germans and 100,000 former Soviets –

Adolf Hitler, seen here giving out medals to Hitler Youth, in his last public appearance, 29 April 1945

Soviet artillery and tank soldiers on Berlin's Kurfürstendamm, once the city's most fashionable boulevard. The Kaiser Wilhelm II church can be seen in the background in this very heavily touched-up Soviet photograph

surrendered in Oslo to General Sir Alfred Thorne. The garrisons left behind on the Channel Islands, Dunkirk, Lorient, San Nazaire and La Rochelle also laid down their arms.

Final Toll

It is not known how many people perished in the Battle of Berlin. Estimates put the number of German dead as high as 200,000 and Russian dead at 150,000. The Soviet troops then went on an orgy of drinking, looting and raping. It is thought that as many as 100,000 women were raped – often publicly and repeatedly – during that period in Berlin. An estimated two million women were raped in the whole of eastern Germany. The Russians sometimes shot their victims afterwards. Other women committed suicide. It is estimated that ten thousand died.

It had been agreed at the Yalta conference in the Crimea in February 1945 that Berlin would be divided between the four powers – Britain, France, the US and the USSR. By the time the Four Power Control Commission arrived to take control the orgy was over. On 4 June, Marshal Zhukov, Field Marshal Montgomery, General Eisenhower and General Jean de Lattre de Tassigny met in Berlin to approve agreements on the occupation, administration and disarmament of Germany. It was also agreed that the principal Nazi war leaders should stand trial before an international court of military justice.

Almost immediately, the Cold War started. The part of the city in the hands of the western powers became West Berlin, an enclave of democracy and free-market capitalism deep inside the region dominated by the Soviet Union which extended a hundred miles to the west of the capital. This was a bone of contention for the next fifty-five years, until the reunification of Germany in 1990.

Chapter 10

THE FAR EAST

While the war against Hitler had been raging in North Africa and Europe, a separate war was being waged against Japan in the Pacific and the Far East. On 8 December 1941, the Japanese attacked the US air base on the Philippines, catching American planes on the ground. The US lost more than half of its B-17 Flying Fortresses and eighty-six other planes. Strategically it was as big a disaster as Pearl Harbor.

After the sinking of the *Prince of Wales* and the *Repulse*, Japanese movement through Malaya was indeed fast and fluid. On 11 January its capital Kuala Lumpur was abandoned to the enemy. By 31 January 1942, all the Commonwealth forces had retreated to Singapore. But the huge guns that defended the island were pointed out to sea. Defences on the landward side, where Japanese troops were threatening, were negligible. By the time Britain surrendered Singapore, on 15 February 1942, its 5 fifteen-inch guns, 6 nine-inch guns and 14 six-inch guns still had not fired a shot.

The loss of HMS *Prince of Wales* and HMS *Repulse*, 10 December 1941: this photograph was taken from a Japanese aircraft during the initial high-level bombing attack. *Repulse*, near the bottom of the view, has just been hit by one bomb and near-missed by several more. *Prince of Wales* is near the top of the image, generating a considerable amount of smoke

Mounted Japanese troops, led by Lieutenant General Sakai, enter Hong Kong on Christmas Day, 1941

Some 85,000 British troops had faced just thirty-thousand Japanese. But the Japanese were led by General Tomoyuki Yamashita, known to his men as 'the Tiger'. The British were led by the ill-starred General Arthur Percival, known among his troops as 'the rabbit'.

The picture of him marching to greet the victorious Japanese with the Union flag held aloft alongside a white flag of surrender revealed the harsh reality that Great Britain no longer had mastery of the seas, nor was she capable of protecting her colonies.

Around eighty-thousand Allied soldiers were taken prisoner, some so newly landed they had not fired a shot. They faced years in the harsh conditions of a Japanese prisoner of war camp – if they survived.

The attack against Hong Kong came on 8 December, just six hours after Pearl Harbor. A request to Lieutenant-General MacArthur, head of US Armed Forces in the Far East, to make an early bombing raid on Japanese air bases on Formosa (Taiwan) was turned down. The garrison of 4,400 Allied troops, including eight-hundred Canadians, held fast until Christmas Day when they were finally overwhelmed by superior Japanese forces.

That same day Japanese forces landed in southern Thailand. Within twenty-four hours the Thai prime minister ordered his forces to end their resistance and within a month had declared war on Britain and America.

Also on 8 December the Japanese had made an initial attack on Wake Island. However, when the invaders returned on 23 December in substantial numbers the US Marines there were compelled to give up the fight. The landings on Borneo began on 15 December and the island fell to the Japanese two weeks later.

On 22 December the Japanese Fourteenth Army landed at Lingayen Gulf on Luzon. Filipino troops of this newly independent nation were no match for the highly trained Japanese. American troops based there withdrew from the capital Manila to mount a defence of the Bataan Peninsula. It was partially successful but bouts of malaria and poor morale left the Americans vulnerable. A Japanese offensive begun on 3 April secured the largest of the Philippine islands within six days.

Those Americans who were capable of escape, numbering in total some 15,000, withdrew to the island of Corregidor. By 9 June all resistance by the Americans and their Filipino allies had ended.

The New Year brought Japan Tarakan, Menado, Rabaul and Timor. Bali, Java and Sumatra were next in line. Where there were defenders, they were swiftly overwhelmed by superior manpower and fighting machines.

On 27 February 1942 came the Battle of the Java Sea, the first genuine naval engagement of the

The British destroy supplies to prevent them falling into Japanese hands during the retreat through Burma

General Sir Archibald Wavell (right), Commander in Chief for India, meeting with General Sir Claude Auchinleck, Commander in Chief for the Middle East, to discuss the war situation, January 1942

war in the Pacific. The Allied fleet lacked air cover and could not match the Long Lance torpedoes possessed by the Japanese. The result was a decisive victory for the Imperial Navy.

The Japanese then turned their attention to Burma, then a British colony. It was rich in raw materials, including rubber, oil and tungsten. A decisive action would sever the Burma Road, an important supply route for the Chinese who were still fighting Japan. It also opened the way to the wealth of British India where the Japanese believed that nationalists would rise up against the British.

Rangoon fell on 8 March and British forces faced the longest retreat in their history as Lieutenant General William Slim followed the Irrawaddy river back to the Indian border, with the Japanese no more than 24 hours behind them. They adopted a

scorched earth policy. According to one estimate, £11 million worth of oil and plant was destroyed in as little as seventy minutes.

Guadalcanal

Buoyed by their success at Midway, the Americans decided to attack Guadalcanal which had fallen to the Japanese in May 1942. The largest of the Solomon Islands, some 90 miles (144 km) long and about 25 miles (40 km) wide, Guadalcanal is 2,500 sq. miles (6,475 sq. km) of tropical rain forest with steep-sided volcanoes and steamy ravines.

The idea of the attack was to prevent Australia and New Zealand being cut off. The Japanese had already demonstrated their hostile intentions towards Australia with an air raid on Darwin on 19 February 1942 by 188 aircraft commanded by Mitsui Fuchida, the man who led the attack on Pearl Harbor. The Japanese were building an airstrip on Guadalcanal.

However, Allied troops were diverted to Papua New Guinea to counter Japanese landings. But on 31 July twenty-three transports and cargo ships set off from Fiji carrying some nineteen-thousand Marines. Naval support was provided by eight cruisers, fifteen destroyers and five high-speed minesweepers. Further out at sea there lay three aircraft carriers, with a battleship, six cruisers, sixteen destroyers and five oilers commanded by Vice Admiral Frank Jack Fletcher.

Fortunately Japanese aircraft had been grounded by poor weather and the island's defenders had no advanced warning of the invasion. When eleven-thousand Marines came ashore on the morning of 7 August, they walked up the beach unopposed. Within twenty-four hours the newly constructed airfield was in American hands along with a considerable quantity of abandoned enemy equipment. The airfield was then renamed Henderson Field after Major Lofton Henderson, an airman killed at Midway. However, at the smaller island of Tulagi, about 20 miles (32 km) away, the defenders fought to almost the last man, claiming the lives of 108 Americans.

Pfc James Donahue recalled his first days on Guadalcanal: 'The jungle is thick as hell. The Fifth regiment landed first and marched to the airport. We went straight through and then cut over to block the escape of the Japs. It took three days to go six miles. Japs took off, left surplus first day which was done away with.

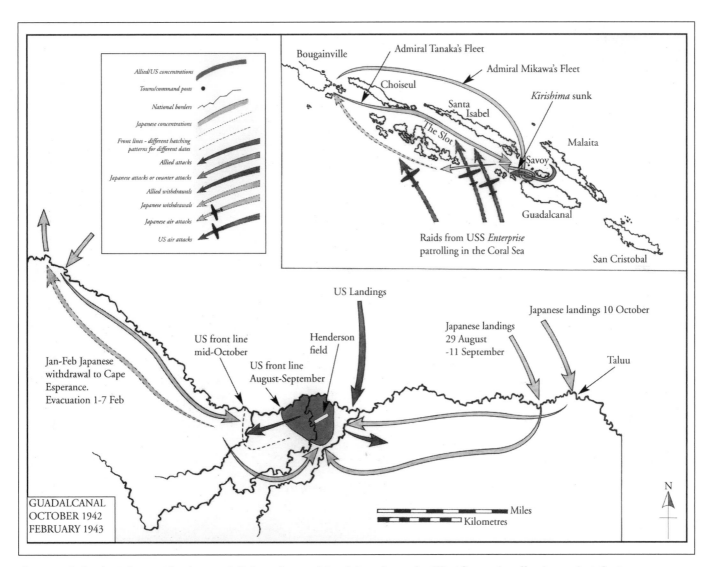

The struggle for the Solomon Islands, especially in and around Guadalcanal, was the Allies' first major offensive against the Japanese

US Marines come ashore on Tulagi Island, 7–8 August 1942. Fighting was fierce as, once again, the Japanese defenders fought to the last man

'The second day was murder. All along the way were discarded packs, rifles, mess gear and everything imaginable. The second night it rained like hell and the bugs were terrible. The Second Battalion had reached the Lunga River. We had to cross four streams.

'The third day we came back. The Japs had beat us in their retreat. We took up beach defence positions. We have been bombed every day by airplanes and a submarine shells us every now and then.

'Our fox holes are four feet (120 cm) deep. We go out on night patrols and it is plenty rugged. We lay in the foxholes for thirteen to fourteen hours at a clip and keep firing at the Japs in the jungles. As yet there is no air support. The mosquitoes are very bad at night. The ants and fleas bother us continually. The planes strafed the beach today. A big naval battle ensued the second day we were here, which

US Marines rest in a jungle clearing on Guadalcanal, circa August–December 1942

resulted in our ship, the *Elliot*, being sunk. All of our belongings were lost…

'Our lieutenant-colonel ambushed and bayoneted. We cleared brush from river for an expected Jap landing. The patrols are going deeper into the jungle each night. They tried to ambush us last night. We are not allowed to fire.'

The Japanese clearly had no intention of permitting a walkover.

> *The Japanese carrier* Ryujo *was torpedoed along with a light carrier, a destroyer and a troop transport. The US carrier* Enterprise *took a couple of hits from Japanese dive-bombers*

Initially, a Japanese attempt to land more ground troops on Guadalcanal by ship from Rabaul came to grief due to a torpedo from a US submarine. However, on 9 August the first in a series of naval battles was a victory for the Japanese. Vice Admiral Gunichi Mikawa brought his ships through The Slot, the waterway between the two strips of islands comprising the Solomons, and, by the light of flares dropped by carrier planes, sank four Allied cruisers in little over twenty minutes in what became known as Ironbottom Sound. Other ships suffered damage and Vice Admiral Fletcher swiftly withdrew his carrier groups from Guadalcanal.

The Eastern Solomons

Before the month was out another major sea battle had been fought. The Battle of the Eastern Solomons involved two aircraft carriers, a light carrier, two

battleships, five cruisers and seventeen destroyers dispatched from the Japanese base at Rabaul in New Britain with the intention of snatching back Guadalcanal. They faced planes from three American carriers. There were considerable losses on both sides. The Japanese carrier *Ryujo* was torpedoed along with a light carrier, a destroyer and a troop transport. The US carrier *Enterprise* took a couple of hits from Japanese dive-bombers. With a plan to land Japanese reinforcements rendered impossible, cautious carrier captains on both sides decided to withdraw under cover of darkness. Then it was left to the Cactus Air Force – the Marine Air Group planes based at Henderson field – to harry Japanese forces. Agile torpedo boats were also used to disrupt the destroyer dashes down the sound that had been dubbed the Tokyo Express.

In a separate incident at the end of August the USS *Saratoga*, one of the key aircraft carriers in the region, was hit by a torpedo and withdrew to Pearl Harbor for repairs. Now, the Japanese had the advantage at sea while the Americans maintained their superiority on land.

The US Naval Construction Force, known as Seabees, laboured to keep Henderson Field open. The first Seabee to receive a war decoration was Seaman 2nd class Lawrence C. Meyer who found and repaired a Japanese machine gun. On 3 October 1942 he used it to shoot down a Japanese Zero attacking the airfield. The award was made posthumously. Less than two weeks later a fuel barge he was working on was hit by Japanese naval gunfire.

In September the Japanese poured thousands of men on to the island. In his diary one Japanese fighter, Genjirous Inui, recorded that, on 6 September, he made a trek over the island during a tropical downpour. 'Having no shelters we slept in the open and Captain and all were soaked to the bone. There are many diarrhoea patients and "the smart of crotch with chaffing" [crotch rot] but the morale of the company is high.'

Soon afterwards he detailed a Japanese operation against tanks aiming to forge a path across Guadalcanal. Gunners opened fire when their targets were 555 yards (500 m) away: 'All the gunners shot tanks one after another, and many tanks were put out of action and went up in flames. They made a counterattack with their cannons and machine guns. But we fired at them at point blank range before the running tanks could find us through their small front view.

A Japanese 'Val' bomber trails smoke as it dives toward USS *Hornet*, 26 October 1942. This plane struck the ship's stack and then her flight deck. The lower aircraft is a 'Kate' shipboard attack plane

'A tank spouted black smoke from the turret, a tank was enveloped in raging flames, a tank set off an explosion in the body and a tank rushed blindly towards us, fell over a precipice on its back and flames poured from the tank. We destroyed ten tanks of fourteen and four retreated into the jungle. The enemy rained down tons of trench mortar shells on our heads. They destroyed one of our guns.'

However, as 14 September dawned, the failure of their considerable efforts on Bloody Ridge was starkly apparent: 'The attack that was carried out full of confidence seems to be a failure. Enemy planes are already taking off safely in the morning. How mortifying! We buried our guns in the sands of the position and went ahead to the gathering point. We had the last ration of rice cut down... for breakfast and we had nothing for lunch.'

While the Americans dug in, Japanese officers told their men: 'It's the time to offer your life for his majesty the Emperor. The flower of Japanese infantrymen is in the bayonet-charge. This is what the enemy soldiers are most afraid of. The strong point of the enemy is superiority of firepower. But it will be able to do nothing in the night and in the jungle. When all-out attack begins, break through the enemy's defences without delay. Recapture our bitterest airfield. Rout, stab, kill and exterminate the enemy before daybreak. We are sure of the ultimate victory of the Imperial Army.'

While bayonet charging did indeed terrify the Americans, they had the weaponry to deal with it.

At sea the US carrier *Wasp* was torpedoed by a submarine on 15 September. Now Vice Admiral William 'Bull' Halsey took charge.

On 13 October Japanese ships shelled the airstrip from the comparative safety of The Slot. Fuel stocks were set on fire and aircraft destroyed.

Japanese losses continued to mount, but the Marines were losing men too. In his journal Donahue wrote: 'A lot of the men were sleeping in their foxholes as a result of working parties during the day and patrols at night. Some of these men were caught unaware by

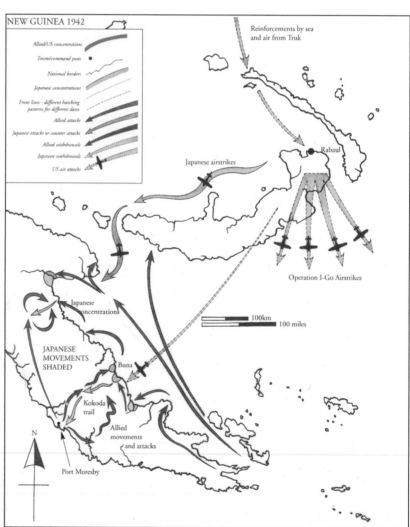

New Guinea was a bloody battleground from the first Japanese attack in 1942 until the end of the war

the Japs who crossed the Lunga River. Corporal K was stabbed by a Jap officer with his sabre right through his face. He then raised his sword and came down on the sleeping corporal. The blow almost severed his leg. It hit him right on the knee bone. K was very powerful and built like a barrel. By this time EDJ, a Frenchman, had woken and attempted to shoot him, but his safety was on and all he could do was parry the Jap's next blow at him. EDJ's hand was cut badly. The Jap officer figured it was too hot for him and started to back away. C, who was about 20 feet (6 m) away, shot him. The next day C got his sword.'

In the battle of Santa Cruz, fought between US and Japanese carrier forces on 26 October, some hundred Japanese aircraft were shot down; seventy-four were lost by the Americans. However, the Japanese succeeded in sinking the US carrier *Hornet*.

On 30 November five US cruisers and six destroyers ambushed a Japanese force using The Slot to deliver supplies to Guadalcanal. However, torpedoes sank an American cruiser and damaged three others while just one Japanese destroyer was sunk.

Nevertheless, in December the Marines on Guadalcanal were finally relieved. By 4 January 1943 the bitter reality had become obvious even to the Japanese high command. The Japanese remaining on Guadalcanal were on starvation rations, prey to innumerable diseases and were incapable of mounting another offensive. For eight days Japanese destroyers slipped along The Slot to pick up eleven thousand men, with a defiant rearguard action fought to prevent attacks by US troops.

By 6 February, when Guadalcanal was finally declared secure, American casualties killed and wounded amounted to six thousand out of a total of sixty-thousand men involved in the fighting. For the Japanese, two thirds of the 36,000 men in action were listed as dead or injured.

With Guadalcanal secure, the Americans had a base to attack the main Japanese south Pacific headquarters at Rabaul.

New Guinea

The Battle of the Coral Sea had ended one Japanese attempt to capture Port Moresby, but Japanese troops landed at Lae and Salamaua on New Guinea in March. Australians landed at Port Moresby and set off along the Kokoda track over the Owen Stanley mountain range to harass the Japanese on the northern shore.

Before the Australians were even close to the coastal village of Buna, some 125 miles (200 km) across country from Port Moresby, the Japanese landed there and sent a sizeable force up the Kokoda track to meet the advancing Australians.

Humidity, steep landscapes, malarial swamps, blades of grass that cut like razors, leeches and incessant rain combined to create one of the worse terrains for warfare. To add to their difficulties Australian servicemen had not been issued with jungle greens and their khaki uniforms made them easy targets.

On 29 July the Japanese captured the village of Kokoda, halfway along the track, forcing the Australians to retreat. The Japanese only halted at the Imita Ridge, just 30 miles (50 km) from Port Moresby. By then, the Allies were devastating the shipping bringing their supplies. Their uniforms rotted on their bodies and some resorted to cannibalism.

By 25 August the Japanese were forced to retreat. But the Australians had no time to celebrate a tactical victory as two thousand Japanese marines were landed at Milne Bay on the eastern tip of New Guinea. They brought with them tanks that got bogged down and they were forced to evacuate.

Back on the Kokoda trail, the Australians were helped by the local Melanesians who acted as porters. They were also supported by Allied fighter planes that strafed the enemy on the narrow mountain paths.

By 2 November the Australians had retaken Kokoda. Now they planned to evict the Japanese from their remaining fortified strongholds at Buna, Gona and Sanananda. With the assistance of fresh Australian and American troops, the battle for Buna was won on 21 January 1943 after a desperate last-ditch stand by the Japanese. There was further mopping up to be done to the east, but the Japanese were no further menace to Port Moresby or Milne Bay.

On New Guinea, the Japanese lost an estimated twelve-thousand men, while the Australians suffered some 5,700 casualties and the Americans 2,800. More Australians died in the Papua New Guinea offensive than in any other during the war. For every battlefield casualty, a further three men had fallen victim to tropical diseases or heat exhaustion.

Australian soldiers pose with a captured Japanese flag after retaking the town of Wau on New Guinea, June 1943

Chapter 11

BURMA

In the closing months of 1942 the British decided to make a thrust back into Burma. This failed with the loss of nine hundred killed and four thousand wounded. The Japanese total casualties were 1,100 with four hundred dead or missing. A Japanese thrust into the malarial territory of Arakan on the Burmese coast in March 1943 was repulsed, but once again British losses were twice those of the Japanese.

Unused to jungle fighting, British morale sagged. The Japanese seemed invincible. The charismatic General William Slim, now in command of the newly-formed Fourteenth Army, saw it as his job to counter this.

Other factors now favoured the British. Supplies came in via the North East India Railways and the RAF had taken delivery of Spitfires and Hurricanes. This gave them mastery of the skies.

In February 1944, while the British planned an attack on the Akyab airfield in Burma, the Japanese launched a surprise attack on a supply and administration base set up by the 7th Indian Division at Sinzewa some distance behind the British lines. The British were encircled and there was bitter fighting around what became known as the 'Admin Box'. The Allied soldiers there were for the most part clerks, mechanics and drivers.

The Allies began parachuting supplies in. Eventually the forces in the box were joined by tanks as British and Indian forces gradually threatened to encircle the Japanese. During the battle of the Admin Box some two thousand tons of food, fuel and ammunition were dropped to the defenders, and more than five thousand casualties were evacuated to India, all for the loss of a single Dakota. With just ten days' supplies, no tanks and no artillery, the Japanese eventually had to pull

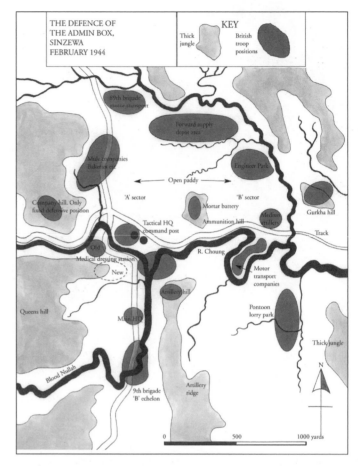

The Japanese attack on Sinzewa

back. They left behind five thousand dead. Britain had won its first victory over the Japanese.

Hoisting the White Flag

What's more, some Japanese soldiers surrendered, a sight Allied soldiers believed they would never see. Each Japanese serviceman had pledged his life to the Emperor and usually preferred suicide to dishonour.

Consequently, Allied soldiers who surrendered to the Japanese were despised by their captors and treated appallingly. Many were dispatched to build the notorious Burma railway, a supply line between Nong Pladuk in Thailand and Thanbyuzayat in Burma. Prisoners worked up to eighteen hours a day to lay a track cut through 260 miles (420 km) of mountainous jungle.

The punishments were vicious; food and sanitation poor. Ulcers refused to heal. Dysentery, malaria, cholera and dehydration were endemic. Men were turned into skin-covered skeletons, their spirit broken. One survivor recalled a fellow soldier who chose to commit suicide by putting his head down a well-soiled latrine and drowning.

Asian labourers brought in from other corners of the empire fared even worse. Some seventy thousand died during the building of the Burma railway, alongside an estimated twelve-thousand British, Australian, American and Dutch. The line was completed in October 1943, bombed by Allied aircraft in 1944 and abandoned in early 1945.

Sabotage Experts

Hugh Trebble, a Royal Air Force clerk taken prisoner in Java, was sent to build a track across Sumatra: 'We had to work sixteen hours a day, seven days a week. We had a bowl of rice in the morning and a bowl of rice at night and it was all we had to live on. At our base camp we used to bury about sixteen men a day. When we were building the railway we were beaten with rails and spanners. The thing to do was to stay conscious. If you fell over and blacked out you were beaten and could get badly injured. One of the guards was so short he would make you stand in a monsoon drain in order to beat you.'

It was a matter of some pride to Trebble and his fellow prisoners that they managed to wreck three steam locomotives in staged accidents.

Many prisoners were transported to the Japanese home islands, including British captain M. P. Murphy captured at Singapore. Excerpts from his diaries highlight the nearly unbearable horrors of the journey made in August 1942 in the hold of a ship.

'My legs are badly swollen right up to the hips with beri beri and am in poor shape after the fever, probably eight and a half stones [119 pounds; 54 kg] at most,' he wrote. 'We were issued with warm suits and what trash! Appears to be made from straw gossamer and pulls apart. No use to anyone.

'We embarked about 12 into hell again, to join a party of about two hundred Americans from the Philippines, the survivors of Bataan and Corregidor – and what a mess of humanity. Shocking, we are bad but they seem much worse and have lost all control from starvation and ill treatment...

'Impossible to describe the foulness. Drinking water rationed and no washing water... Seems impossible that we can survive this awful filth for long. Food, dysentery, fever, no means of keeping anything clean. Latrine accommodation only three cubicles for 2,500 and with the dysentery and diarrhoea...'

About twenty died on the six-day journey.

The Chindits

Orthodox military thinking had failed in Burma. So Colonel Orde Wingate formed the Long Range Penetration Group who became known as the Chindits. Initially the force comprised the 77th Infantry Brigade made up of the 13th King's (Liverpool) Regiment, 3/2nd Ghurka Rifles, 142 Commando Company, 2nd Burma Rifles, eight RAF sections, a Brigade signal section from the Royal Corps of Signals and a mule transport company. Wingate himself came up with the distinctive name, derived from the word for the winged creatures said to guard Burmese pagodas, *chinthe*.

The Chindits left India on 8 February 1943 to cut the railway line between Mandalay and Myitkyina

A Chindit column crossing a Burmese river, deep in enemy territory, 1943. Through their tactical successes behind enemy lines, the Chindits showed that the much-feared Japanese army could be taken on and defeated

and disrupt the enemy behind their lines. Again they were supplied by airdrops.

Depleted Forces

Having achieved their objectives, Wingate was ordered to withdraw on 24 March. By then, many of the men were weak due to illness, exhaustion and poor nutrition, and the journey back over the Chindwin and Irrawaddy rivers remained treacherous. Out of three thousand officers and men that set out from Imphal four months earlier just 2,182 returned in May and June, having walked between 1,000 and 1,500 miles (1,600–2,400 km). Only about a quarter remained fighting fit. Despite the losses, the propaganda value was immense.

A second expedition was organized for March 1944. This time, the equivalent of six brigades was employed rather than one as in the first outing. Again aerial drops were going to be key to survival.

Churchill described the launch of the second Chindit campaign in a letter to Roosevelt, with two Long Range Penetration brigades landing in the jungle 100 miles (160 km) inside enemy territory: 'The first landings were made by gliders, whose occupants then prepared the strips to receive transport aircraft. Between 6 March and 11 March seven thousand five hundred men, with all their gear and with mules, were successfully landed. The only losses were a number of the gliders and some of these should be reparable.

'The brigades have now started their advance but a small holding party has been left at one of the strips to receive a flight of Spitfires and a squadron of Hurricanes which were to fly in to protect the base and provide air support.

'The only serious mishap occurred on the first night. One of the strips in the northern area was found to have been obstructed by the Japanese, and the surface of the remaining strip was much worse than was expected, causing crashes which blocked the strip and prevented further landings that night. A few of the gliders had to be turned back in the air and failed to reach our territory. Another strip was immediately prepared in this area and was ready for landing two days later. The total of killed, wounded and missing is at most 145.'

On 25 March, just weeks into the second campaign the charismatic Wingate was killed in an air crash. Nevertheless, the guerrilla techniques he pioneered served the British well.

Bombed entrance to a tunnel where British and Indian troops captured a major highway

The Simple Life

'Life in the Chindits was extremely simple,' recalled Rodney Tatchell of the Royal Engineers. 'To prepare oneself for bed one simply spread a groundsheet, took off one's boots, made a pillow of one's pack and one's inflated "Mae West" and rolled oneself in one's blanket. Getting up was just the reverse procedure. It was often anything up to three weeks before one had the chance of an all-over wash in a stream. From December 1943 to May 1944 I never slept on anything but the ground with just the sky above – if you could see it through the roof of the jungle.'

On 13 May 1944, 47 Column were ambushed in their bivouac by a patrol from the Japanese 53rd Division. Two officers, a sergeant major and six privates were killed. A further thirteen men were wounded, including Harold Lambert who had been shot in the lower leg.

'There was a hell of a racket,' he recalled. 'Some were still asleep, others were brewing up when all hell let loose. At first I didn't realize how badly I'd been wounded. I was more concerned for the mule that was carrying all the column's money – it was so badly wounded it had to be shot. A major tried to lead a counter attack but as he stood up he fell dead with a bullet through the head. We then dispersed further into the jungle. I was lucky as I could still walk after a fashion. Lots of Japanese were killed and as we scrambled up a steep mountainside and over a river we lost lots of mules, either through falls or drowning.'

The column swiftly regrouped and soon made contact with another column from Nigerian brigades further west. Eventually Lambert was evacuated by light aircraft from an airstrip on the shores of Lake Inawgyi.

Although they were only lightly armed – their biggest weapons being medium machine guns and three-inch mortars – if they needed something more powerful, all they had to do was to call up air base for dive-bombers, mark the target with a mortar smoke bomb and American Mustangs would blast hell out of the opposition.

Again the Chindits were a costly nuisance to the Japanese. The second Chindit expedition was just a week too late to hamper the Japanese attack on Imphal. However, the first expedition pressured Lieutenant General Renya Mutaguchi into rushing his preparations for an attack into India. The result was a costly failure.

Imphal and Kohima

Despite the setbacks they were experiencing elsewhere in 1944, the Japanese remained convinced India could still be theirs. In March

The battle for Kohima

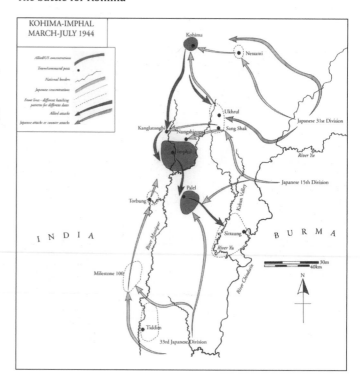

1944 the Japanese Fifteenth Army, numbering some 155,000, under the command of Lieutenant General Mutaguchi breached the Indian border and headed for the British outposts at Imphal and Kohima for a twin-pronged assault.

When Japanese intentions became clear, the British forces at Imphal were swiftly reinforced by the 5th Indian Division. They were joined by the 7th Indian Division and other stray brigades that could be pulled in. Even a brigade of Chindits joined the battle.

The invading Japanese were soon short of equipment as their supply lines were long and subject to attack. About half the supplies for the Indian campaign never made it that far thanks to British and American submarines, bombers and saboteurs.

The Japanese were supported in their attack by the Indian National Army, comprising Indian nationalists, former prisoners of war who had fought for the British, led by Chandra Bose. On 14 April 1944 the INA was able to hoist the Indian tricolor flag above Indian soil for the first time. Soon Japanese artillery was firmly entrenched in the surrounding hilltops and pointing at Imphal.

Who Controls Kohima, Controls the Pass

Some 80 miles (130 km) from Imphal, Kohima was some 5,000 feet (1,500 m) above sea level and controlled the pass in the Assam valley. Holding the defences were the 161st Indian Brigade, comprising the 4th Royal West Kents, 1/1st Punjabis and the 4/7th Rajputs, with a contingent of the Assam Rifles and Assam Regiment, with troops from the 5th and 7th Indian Divisions arriving by air to reinforce them later.

Men of the West Yorkshire Regiment and 10th Gurkha Rifles advance along the Imphal-Kohima road behind Lee-Grant tanks, March/April 1944

Fierce fighting erupted between the British and Japanese on 23 March. By 4 am on 5 April, the Japanese had managed to reach the outskirts of Kohima. Their aim was to cut the links between Kohima and Imphal then surround the town.

One of two Victoria Crosses awarded during the battle of Kohima went to Lance Corporal John Harman of the Royal West Kents. When he spotted a Japanese light machine gun team taking over a nearby trench, he sprinted some 35 yards (32 m) towards the trench, flung a grenade which killed the two Japanese inside and returned to his line bearing a captured gun.

Two days later on 9 April in cold, wet weather he repeated this astonishing performance only this time there were five men in the trench armed with automatic weapons and he himself used a fixed bayonet rather than a grenade. When all the enemy were dead he walked back to his lines, ignoring his comrades' pleas to run for cover. He was killed by a burst of fire and died, saying: 'I've got to go. It was worth it – I got the lot.'

While this was happening Corporal Taffy Rees stood up, was hit twice and rolled into a no man's land. Another soldier who tried to rescue him was hit twice with bullets. Rees lay there paralyzed. Soon he was delirious and for eight hours he was screaming, shouting and calling for his mum and

An Indian soldier using smoke grenades to clear Japanese troops from bunkers in the Maungdaw hills, during Fourteenth Army's advance, 1944.

dad and praying, until he died. There was nothing anyone could do about it.

Playing for High Stakes

By 9 April the British and Indian defenders were isolated. The following day their field supply depot was being raided by the Japanese. However, the British were aided by the local Naga tribesmen who gathered intelligence for them.

By 13 April the chief battleground was the District Commissioner's bungalow and his tennis court, which became a treacherous 'no man's land' with the lines entrenched on either side and grenades being lobbed over it.

The battle diary of 4 Battalion Royal West Kents from 13 April reads: 'The Japs made a heavy rush attack at B Coy from the DC bungalow and succeeded in penetrating into a shed on a small but important hillock when a Bren [gun] jammed... Lt King restored the situation by driving them out with grenades but not before the Bren gunner himself picked up a shovel and cracked at his assailants with it.'

Next day the diary notes another attack 'repulsed with many casualties to the enemy'. The defenders successfully received an air drop of water. Meanwhile the Japanese use of smoke bombs indicated that their stocks of ammunition were now running low. They were also being pounded by artillery positions to the west of Kohima.

The defenders had been pushed on to a ridge and were attacked from all sides. For 16 days in April 1944 they held out, assisted by parachute drops and aerial raids on the enemy. Finally, on 20 April, relief came in the form of the 161st Indian Infantry Brigade fighting through from Dimapur with the 2nd British Division. The Japanese onslaught could not be sustained.

Tank driver Herbet Adderley with 149 Royal Armoured Corps recalled going into Kohima, driving a leading tank behind enemy lines. The crews of five tanks dispatched previously that day had all perished after the commanding officer had panicked. Adderley's tank was armed with a Thompson sub-machine gun that none of the crew had used before. The tank was soon hit by enemy fire.

'The order to bail out came,' said Adderley. 'I asked the gun loader to just open the door two inches (5 cm) so that I could see. He pressed the handle down, the weight of the door pulled out of his fingers and shot wide open. Christ Almighty. Two trenches of Japanese were about 100 feet (30 m) away with their guns lined up on us. They were expecting us to come out of the turret where the commander would be. It gave us a few seconds. I pressed the trigger [of the submachine gun] but I could hardly hold it. It was going up and down like something alive as it was difficult to hold but they dropped out of sight. I was out of that tank like a blue bottle fly and behind the tank. The rest of the crew was following.'

Nearby they saw the body of the commanding officer. Adderley turned him over and saw his eyes begin to flicker.

Japanese Retreat

The column then advanced from Kohima to Imphal, despite monsoon conditions and poor visibility. But the Japanese had already been ordered to abandon the operation and were on their way back to Burma, leaving behind 3,800 dead.

The clearance of Kohima took some weeks. During that time sniper and grenades duels continued. Bayonets and flamethrowers also found a use.

The second Victoria Cross was won by Temporary Captain John Randle of 2 Battalion, The Royal Norfolk Regiment, who had refused to be evacuated even though he was wounded. On 6 May he led his men forward to capture a hilltop vantage point then saw that a neighbouring bunker remained in the hands of the Japanese. In the face of enemy fire he charged this bunker, threw a grenade inside and then flung his body across the opening, ensuring all inside would die.

By July the Japanese pulled out of India, pursued relentlessly by Allied armies and air forces. They fought one another for food, stripped walking boots from the sick and drowned in great numbers...

In the air the Air Transport Command – comprising both the RAF and the USAAF – was at full stretch as they knew the lives of the men in battle depended on them. They were also supplying the Chinese army, flying 'over the hump' – the Himalayas – on a route known as The Aluminium Trail because it was littered with so much wreckage.

A UK Ministry of Defence report estimated that 19,000 tons of supplies were delivered by the RAF during the battle of Kohima. In addition it airlifted twelve thousand men in, and thirteen thousand casualties as well as 43,000 non-combatants out. It also carried fourteen million bags of rations, 1,200 bags of mail, 43 million cigarettes and one million gallons of petrol.

After the withdrawal from Kohima, remaining troops had been diverted to Imphal for what Mutaguchi called a 'do or die' assault. They died in droves, not least for the want of decent supplies. Outraged, General Kotoku Sato telegraphed his boss: 'The tactical ability of the Fifteenth Army staff lies below that of cadets.' He began a retreat to save the remnants of his forces. When Mutaguchi began to question his troop movements, Sato cut the communications wires.

Lifting the Siege

The siege of Imphal was lifted on 22 June when the road from Kohima was finally cleared of enemy forces. The Allies now had tanks while the Japanese had no anti-tank weaponry. By July the Japanese pulled out of India, pursued relentlessly by Allied armies and air forces. They fought one another for food, stripped walking boots from the sick and dying, and drowned in great numbers in the swollen waters of River Chindwin. The most feeble were left to blow themselves up with grenades.

Some thirty-thousand Japanese soldiers out of a force of 85,000 were killed. A further 23,000 were wounded. Men on both sides were traumatized by thirst, hunger and tropical diseases. Yet for the Allied soldiers there was some relief in terms of fresh water, food and medicines dropped by low flying transport planes and this proved the key for the Allied operation that would win back Burma.

Over the next year, an Allied army of British, American, Indian, African and Chinese troops chased the Japanese across Burma, avoiding large-scale engagements and letting tropical diseases do their worst. In the final two months alone, twenty thousand of the remaining 27,000 perished. The total number of Allied casualties in the same period stood at ninety-five. By then, the bombing of the Japanese home islands had made Burma a backwater.

Chapter 12

ISLAND HOPPING

After Guadalcanal, American attention turned to Rabaul, by far the most important Japanese base in the region.

They began a two-pronged assault with General MacArthur clearing the Huon peninsula in New Guinea, while Admiral Halsey moved up through the Solomons.

By the time they had managed to reach Rabaul, it had been virtually evacuated. So they bypassed the port and moved on.

The Aleutian Islands

The Aleutian Islands of Attu and Kiska had been occupied by the Japanese since June 1942. On 11 May 1943 the 7th US Infantry Division landed on Attu amid aerial bombardments from aircraft carrier planes. After two weeks dogged resistance, the Japanese resorted to suicidal charges that over-ran two command posts and a medical station. In the end, the Americans took just twenty-eight pris-

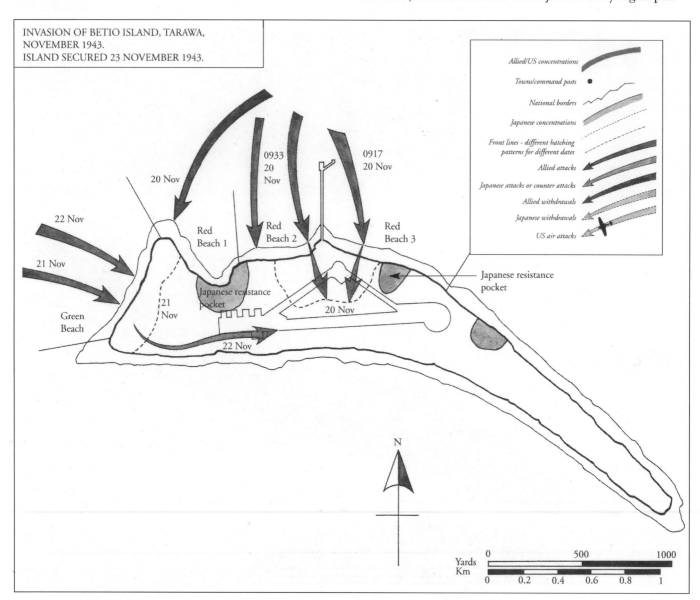

INVASION OF BETIO ISLAND, TARAWA, NOVEMBER 1943.
ISLAND SECURED 23 NOVEMBER 1943.

Allied/US concentrations
Towns/command posts
National borders
Japanese concentrations
Front lines - different hatching patterns for different dates
Allied attacks
Japanese attacks or counter attacks
Allied withdrawals
Japanese withdrawals
US air attacks

20 Nov

22 Nov

21 Nov

Green Beach

Red Beach 1

0933 20 Nov

Red Beach 2

0917 20 Nov

Red Beach 3

Japanese resistance pocket

21 Nov

Japanese resistance pocket

20 Nov

22 Nov

N

Yards
Km
0   500   1000
0   0.2   0.4   0.6   0.8   1

When the Americans came ashore in their amphibious vehicles at Betio Island, they were about to encounter ferocious resistance. Over 6,000 Japanese, Koreans and Americans died in the fighting that followed

US Marines of the 2nd Division come ashore on Betio Island, Tarawa. The Japanese garrison was well entrenched in the rock of the island, and would resist to the last man

oners while a total of 2,351 Japanese bodies were found. American casualties amounted to six hundred dead and 1,200 wounded. With some trepidation the US forces under Vice Admiral Thomas Kincaid set about trying to secure Kiska, initially with a sea blockade and aerial bombardments. However, under a blanket of fog, the Japanese evacuated. On 15 August, 34,000 US and Canadian troops made an amphibious assault. More than fifty were killed in friendly fire incidents before it was established that the enemy had gone.

Operation Galvanic
Now the target for the Allies was the Gilbert and Marshall Islands between the Solomons and Hawaii. Operation Galvanic with the twin objectives of Makin and Tarawa began on 20 November 1943, following a comprehensive bombardment from both aircraft and battleships.

At Makin a 6,472-man invasion force got the better of 848 defenders in four days. It was a different story at the Tarawa atoll. On the main island of Betio, 4,500 elite Japanese troops had dug themselves in, in an area the size of New York's Central Park. The Japanese commander, Rear-Admiral Shibasaki Keiji claimed that one million men thrown at them for one hundred years still would not triumph. The area was saturated by bombing but its fortified positions survived. When the 2nd Marine Division waded ashore, so many were cut down it looked like the American forces would be tossed back into the sea.

However, a communications breakdown prevented a full-on Japanese counterattack on the first night. In turn that allowed the Marines to establish positions ashore. Reinforcements ultimately overwhelmed the Japanese, who resorted once again to banzai charges.

While the Japanese were all but wiped out, the Americans lost 1,009 dead and 2,101 wounded.

Operation Flintlock

Next in line were the Marshall Islands, mandated to Japan after World War I. The invasion force that was marshalled in Operation Flintlock comprised some 85,000 men and nearly three-hundred warships, transports and landing craft.

On 30 January 1944 the landings

A rare image of Japanese prisoners, taken on Betio Island. Most Japanese soldiers considered death infinitely preferable to the dishonour of surrender

American troops storm Japanese positions on Kwajalein

began on Kwajalein, the world's largest atoll. Some 36,000 shells were fired in preparation for the landings. As a result, in the end, some 8,400 Japanese lay dead compared to 500 Americans.

Other atolls were bombed and bypassed. By 23 February Eniwetok atoll was also in US hands. Truk, further to the west in the Carolines, was attacked for the first time using radar-guided night bombing. After a naval bombardment, the Marines took over the atoll. Most of its 3,500 Japanese defenders were killed. Now a strategically

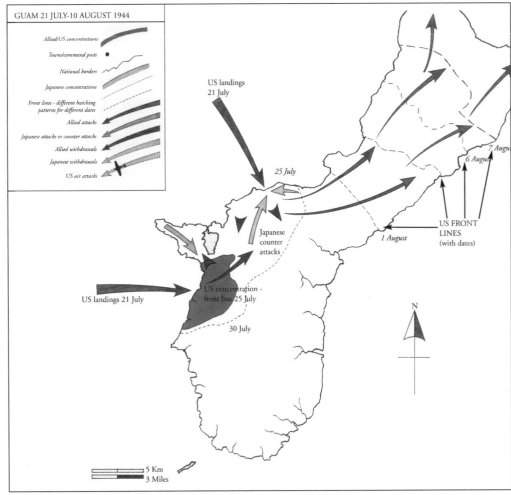

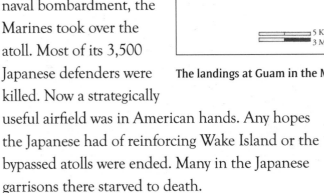

The landings at Guam in the Marianas Islands

useful airfield was in American hands. Any hopes the Japanese had of reinforcing Wake Island or the bypassed atolls were ended. Many in the Japanese garrisons there starved to death.

The Marianas

The Marianas are a group of mountainous islands in the West Pacific ocean that include Tinian, Saipan and Guam. Lying just 1,200 miles (1,900 km) south of Japan, their strategic importance was immense. With the capture of the Marianas Islands the Americans would have control of an airbase from which they could strike Japan.

The first target was Saipan. The US task force, comprising eight-hundred ships and twenty-eight submarines, left Majuro in the Marshall Islands on 6 June 1944, buoyed by news of the Normandy landings. The landings on Saipan were scheduled for the 15th.

The battle for Saipan was long and bitter. The Marines were reinforced by the US Army's 27th Infantry Division, and together they hounded the Japanese into a corner. On 7 July about three-thousand Japanese committed themselves to a banzai charge that – inevitably – ran out of manpower within twenty-four hours. By 10 July Saipan was secure.

On Saipan there were a large number of Japanese civilians. Many threw themselves from cliff tops often with their children in their arms. Nothing could dissuade them. Two out of every three Japanese civilians on the island chose to die. In all, some 29,000 Japanese perished while 16,525 Americans were killed and wounded.

The Battle of the Philippine Sea

While the battle raged on Saipan, the war's biggest battle between carriers was being waged at sea. The First Japanese Mobile Fleet commanded by Vice-Admiral Jizaburo Ozawa took on the Fifth US Fleet under Admiral Raymond A. Spruance.

The Japanese had hoped to destroy a third of the American craft with its land-based aircraft and submarines. This ambition was thwarted when seventeen out of twenty-five Japanese submarines were sunk and the airstrips earmarked for the action were wrecked by bombing.

Initially, Ozawa held the advantage because the Americans had no idea where he was. But when he broke radio silence to order aerial bombardments, the US fleet was able to send up sufficient aircraft to thwart the attack. Only 130 aircraft out of 373 survived. Along with a further fifty Japanese aircraft

B-17 bomber of the USAAF on a bombing run over the Solomon Islands, preparatory to the US assault on New Guinea, October 1942

lost over Guam, this was known as 'The Great Marianas Turkey Shoot'. Meanwhile the Japanese lost the carriers *Taiho* and *Shokaku* to torpedo strikes.

Then Task Force 58, under the command of Vice-Admiral Marc Mitscher, set out in pursuit of the Japanese fleet and launched a carrier aircraft strike that took out the carrier *Hiya* and damaged two others. Hampered by lack of fuel and dark skies about eighty US aircraft got into difficulties on return, although most of their crews were saved. However, the Japanese were left with just thirty-five carrier aircraft.

Guam

On 21 July, the 3rd Marine Division and the 1st Marine Brigade of General Turner's Joint Expeditionary Force landed at Agat and Asan on Guam, north and south respectively of the Orote Peninsula. Again, relatively easy landings were followed by savage fighting against a fanatical enemy, well dug into the hillsides and rugged terrain of the island. It ended with the now familiar banzai charges, the defenders of the 18,000-strong garrison preferring to sacrifice their lives rather than surrender. While resistance was over by 10 August, the last Japanese

USS *Bunker Hill* is near-missed by a Japanese bomb, during the air attacks of 19 June 1944. The Japanese plane, with its tail shot off, is about to crash, at left

soldiers on Guam, hidden in the rough ground of the north of the island, did not finally surrender until 1972, twenty-eight years later.

The Bombing of Japan

The Americans quickly built runways in the Marianas Islands and on 4 February 1945 70 Boeing B-29 Superfortresses dropped 160 tons of incendiaries upon the city of Kobe. Most of its buildings were made of wood and they blazed instantly. Similar treatment was dished out to Tokyo on 25 February when 450 tons of incendiaries destroyed an estimated 28,000 buildings.

In March the bombers came at lower altitudes and at night to create firestorms similar to those seen in German cities. People died by the thousand and the terror among the survivors was immense. Journalist Masuo Kato recalled his nephew Kozo Ishikawa who 'held an unshakeable faith in Japanese victory. To his small world it was unthinkable that the Emperor's armies could suffer defeat or that the Japanese navy should endure any fate other than glorious victory.

'After his home was burned to the ground during a B-29 raid, destroying almost every familiar material thing that had made up his existence, he told me with great gravity: "We cannot beat the B-29."

He became ill and died shortly after the war was over from what a doctor called a nervous breakdown.

The raids continued throughout the spring of 1945. When Tokyo had been laid to waste, Major General Curtis Le May turned his attentions to other cities, frequently dropping leaflets warning of an impending raid, further driving down morale among a hungry and increasingly desperate population.

The War Under the Sea

As well as attacking Japanese warships, American submarines also targeted merchant shipping to deprive the Japanese war machine of raw materials. At the beginning of 1944, the Japanese had the use of 4.1 million tons of merchant shipping, excluding tankers. By the end of the year that had been reduced by more than half. In September of that year some 700,000 tons of shipping transported oil around the empire. Four months later, the figure had been reduced to 200,000. By 1945 the supplies of oil reaching Japan were almost non-existent, crippling both the economy and the war effort.

The Japanese also had submarines, but their use was restricted to raids along the coasts of Australia and America. Later Japanese submarines were used to transport men and supplies to the battlefront rather than striking at the enemy. During the war the US lost fifty-two submarines out of a force of 288 while the Japanese losses totalled 128 submarines out of two hundred.

Japanese cargo ship the *Nittsu Maru* sinking in the Yellow Sea, off China, on 23 March 1943. Periscope photograph, taken from USS *Wahoo*, which had torpedoed her

The Battle of Leyte Gulf

The invasion of the Philippines was scheduled for 20 October 1944. This was a matter for personal rejoicing for General MacArthur, evicted ignominiously from the Philippines earlier in the war. But first Peleliu, in the Palau islands in the approaches to the Philippines, had to be taken.

The Americans believed the island to be lightly defended. And so it appeared to be when Marines landed on 12 September 1944. Once they were ashore the Japanese put up tenacious resistance. After a week the 1st Marines were down to half their combat strength and the casualties in the 5th and 7th Marines accounted for more than four out of every ten men sent ashore. Some twelve-thousand Japanese had died. Peleliu measured just 6 miles long and 2 miles wide (9 by 3 km) and was of questionable strategic value.

However, America's intentions were now clear. At its disposal Japan only had the remnants of its once fine fleet and the lucky survivors of its air arm. Nevertheless, the aim was to attack the invasion fleet as it landed men on to the island of Leyte. To do so, half the strike force led by Vice Admiral Takeo Kurita was to approach the target area from the north while the rest came from the south. Meanwhile another flotilla led by Admiral Ozawa would lure American shipping into action so they would be too far away to assist the invasion force at Leyte. The operation was called *Sho-Go* or Victory.

It failed because two American submarines had spotted Kurita's force in the Palawan Passage. He had halted the customary zig-zigging of the Japanese ships to conserve fuel. In the early hours of 23 October, American torpedoes sank two heavy cruisers and badly damaged a third.

Battle of the Sibuyan Sea

On 24 October aircraft from Task Force 38 (3rd Fleet) discovered Kurita's forces in the Sibuyan Sea. A first wave of US aircraft was driven off by Japanese planes and anti-aircraft fire from the ships.

The Japanese flag ships *Musashi* and *Yamoto* suffered a series of torpedo and bomb hits during this encounter but sailed on. Then as the bombardment continued the *Musashi* was left limping and slipped to the ocean bottom, the victim of twenty torpedo and seventeen bomb hits.

Kurita reversed his course, making the US pilots think he was pulling out of the battle altogether.

> *After a week the 1st Marines were down to half their combat strength and the casualties in the 5th and 7th Marines accounted for more than four out of every ten men sent ashore*

Land-based Japanese bombers wreaked a revenge of sorts by hitting the carrier *Princeton* and damaging a cruiser and five destroyers. Then the feint drawn up by the Japanese navy column led by Ozawa – to lure the 3rd Fleet away from Leyte – swung into action. Halsey took the bait. Now the Japanese could execute a pincer movement and destroy the forces at Leyte Gulf, all of which had their guns pointing towards shore.

However, in the evening of 24 October one prong of the Japanese attack force encountered six US battleships, four heavy and four light cruisers accompanied by destroyers strung out along the Surigao Strait. In the battle that followed the

Japanese commander Vice Admiral Shoji Nishimura was killed and his flagship *Yamashiro* was sunk. Only two ships in Nishimura's force survived.

The second prong under Kurita slipped through the San Bernardino Strait into the Philippine Sea under cover of darkness without being noticed. Some 15 miles (24 km) ahead lay six escort carriers. Battle commenced off the island of Samar in the early hours of 25 October. He sank two Allied escort carriers and three destroyers, but then retired after counter-attacks led him to believe that the force ranged against him was greater than it was. Had he stayed, Kurita might well have wrecked the largest amphibious landing yet in the Pacific.

Halsey sent back a task force although it arrived too late to be of help. But at the ensuing Battle of Cape Engamo, Halsey picked off four carriers and a destroyer.

For the Americans, the Battle of Leyte Gulf was a success and its maritime supremacy was now assured, while the Imperial Japanese Navy, once thought to be invincible, no longer had the capacity to protect the home islands.

On the shore the invasion of Leyte had begun on 20 October. The assault forces landed 202,500 troops on Leyte from five hundred ships. Within four days two important airbases had fallen, but the runways were damaged and it was not until 3 December that Marine F6F-3N Hellcats could be landed there to provide air cover for the fighting men.

Meanwhile, the garrison on Leyte was being reinforced by the Japanese and the fifteen-thousand defenders became sixty thousand. The Americans

Japanese aircraft carrier *Zuikaku* (centre) and two destroyers under attack by US Navy carrier aircraft, 20 June 1944. Although hit by several bombs during these attacks, *Zuikaku* survived

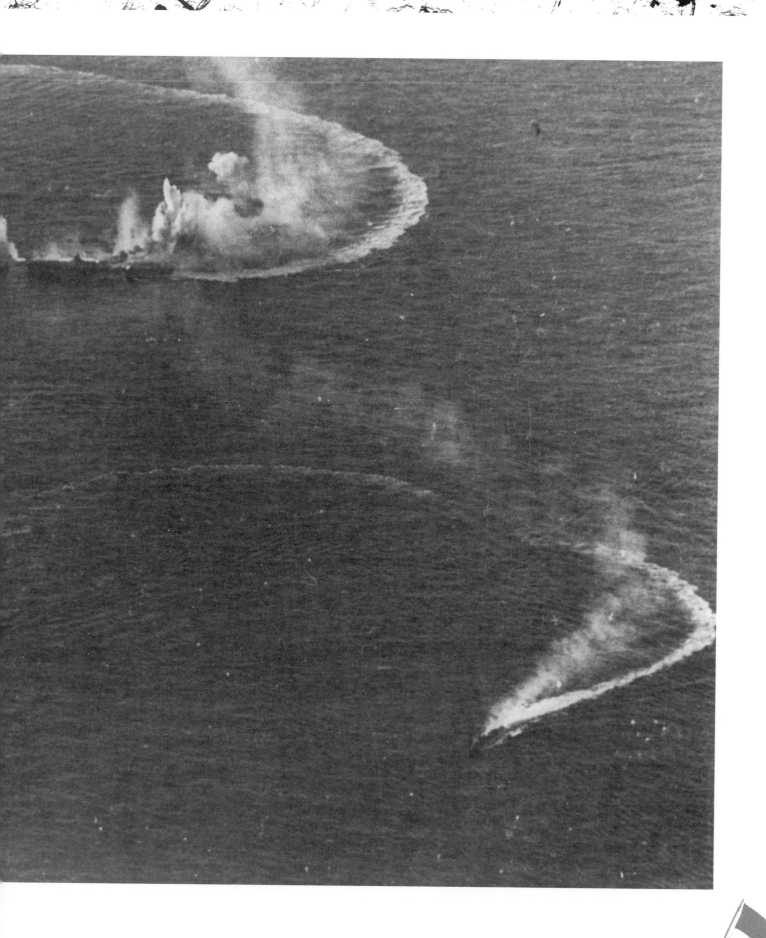

were further held up by seasonal rainfall. However, the Japanese were unable to turn the tide of Americans as naval action against shipping from Manila meant supplies soon dried up.

As early as mid November, the Japanese commander General Yamashita conceded that Leyte was lost and that Luzon, the larger, neighbouring island, would soon be as well, though his defensive actions succeeded in delaying the attack on Luzon until 9 January.

Approaching Luzon from Lingayen, the same place the Japanese had themselves landed, the American invasion was subject to suicide attacks by kamikaze pilots.

The Divine Wind

The word 'kamikaze' translates as 'divine wind' and refers to the typhoon that prevented the invasion of Japan by Mongol warlord Genghis Khan in 1281. In the Pacific war, the kamikaze turned their plane and themselves into a powerful weapon. The slogan was 'one plane, one warship'.

When Vice Admiral Takijirio Onishi realized a vast US naval fleet was heading for the Philippines he knew, if the Philippines fell, that the next stop would be the Japanese home islands. Dubbed 'father of the kamikaze', he explained to his troops: 'There is only one way of channelling our meagre strength into maximum efficiency and that is to

Crew members of the sinking carrier *Zuikaku* give a final 'banzai' cheer after the Japanese Naval Ensign is lowered during the afternoon of 25 October

Kamikaze pilots attend a final briefing by a senior officer before heading off on their one-way trip

organize suicide attack units composed of Zero fighters equipped with 250 kilogram bombs, with each plane to crash-dive into an enemy carrier.'

Before the end of the war, between four thousand and seven thousand Japanese pilots, mostly aged between twenty and twenty-two, although some were as young as seventeen, flew one-way operations. According to Allied records the kamikaze campaign claimed thirty-four escort carriers and a further 288 ships were seriously damaged. The death toll among the Allied servicemen came to more than three thousand and twice as many were wounded.

No matter how enthusiastically a kamikaze embraced his task he was still chained into the cockpit and drugged before take-off to prevent the natural urge for self-preservation to kick in. Those committed to death hoped to bring a measure of

The flight deck of the aircraft carrier *Bunker Hill*, while her crew fight fires caused by kamikaze hits off Okinawa, 11 May 1945

US tanks roll ashore from LCTs (Landing Craft, Tank) on Lingayen Gulf Beach, Luzon, January 1945

glory to themselves and their family. Among their fellow pilots they were known as the Sons of Heaven, or even 'gods without earthly desires'. In his last letter, one wrote: 'When you hear that I have died after sinking an enemy ship, I hope you will have kind words to say about my gallant death.'

Each wore a white knotted scarf around their necks, a headband recalling one worn in the days when the warrior Samurai class dominated and a cloth stitched with the hair of a thousand women – thought to be lucky.

Ultimately the surrender of the Emperor released the surviving kamikaze from their death oath. Onishi then killed himself in the traditional manner of hara kiri, disembowelling himself with a sword.

After Leyte was captured the island of Mindoro fell within a few days. But during the invasion of Luzon sixteen ships were lost to the kamikazes in a single day. The cruiser *Australia* was hit five times in four days but remained in action.

Elsewhere the US navy was unmolested and spread out from the Philippines into the South China Sea in January, hitting targets as distant as Saigon and Hong Kong.

Strong Japanese forces on Luzon were attacked not only by Americans but also by Filipino guerrillas who risked much to join a battle of liberation. This came too late to prevent American prisoners of war being shipped to the home islands. Their ships were subject to air attack. Two ships were sunk, and at least one other was seriously damaged by a shell that killed dozens of prisoners penned in already appalling conditions below deck.

Manila was cleared of Japanese forces by house-to-house combat. By the time the city fell to the US on 4 March 1945, sixteen-thousand Japanese lay dead. It took several more months to clear the rest of the significant Philippine islands of Japanese defenders. It was not until 2 September, long after any realistic hope of victory had vanished, that Yamashita finally surrendered, along with about fifty-thousand men, all close to starvation.

Iwo Jima and Okinawa

The Americans' island-hopping strategy continued and the next target was Iwo Jima, just 650 miles (1,050 km) from Tokyo. The island was just 5 miles long and two-and-a-half miles (8 by 4 km) wide. It was packed full of Japanese veteran fighters who had been instructed to fight to the death. Reinforcements were dug in deep in the soft volcanic rock. One of the labyrinths was 75 feet (23 m) deep and could hold two thousand troops. They were armed with heavy and medium artillery, anti-aircraft batteries, heavy and light machine guns, mortars and tanks.

The struggle for Okinawa

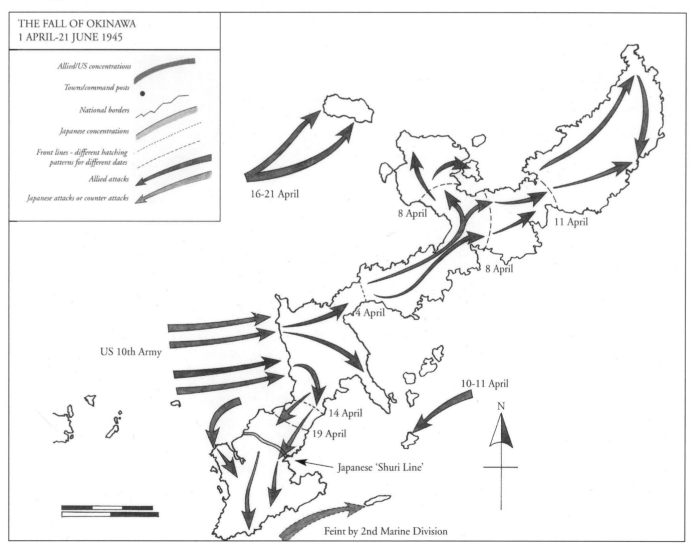

THE FALL OF OKINAWA
1 APRIL-21 JUNE 1945

Allied/US concentrations
Towns/command posts
National borders
Japanese concentrations
Front lines - different hatching patterns for different dates
Allied attacks
Japanese attacks or counter attacks

16-21 April

8 April

11 April

8 April

4 April

10-11 April

US 10th Army

14 April

19 April

Japanese 'Shuri Line'

N

Feint by 2nd Marine Division

US Marines of 4th Division take cover from enemy fire on the shores of Iwo Jima, 19 February 1945. A US battleship and amphibious vehicles are docked on the beach

For several months before the invasion the island was bombarded by carrier aircraft and the naval guns. But this had little effect on the underground defenders.

On the morning of 19 February 1945, an armada of 450 ships of the US 5th Fleet assembled off Iwo Jima. A total of 482 assorted landing craft brought the men of eight US Marine battalions ashore, with the first wave hitting the beach at about 9 am. They landed almost unopposed. It was only when they broached the first sand ridge that they were cut down by gunfire from Japanese snipers hidden in caves. Each Japanese soldier was tasked with killing ten Americans. On the first day, 566 US Marines lay dead or dying. However, some thirty thousand were ashore by the end of the day, already outnumbering the Japanese.

But the Marines remained hemmed in to a small beachhead under almost perpetual fire. Soon the Japanese found themselves running short of ammunition as well as fresh water.

Raising the Flag

On the morning of 23 February Marines from Company E in the 2nd Battalion survived the treacherous climb to the top of Mount

US Marines plant the 'stars and stripes' on the summit of Mount Suribachi. This was not, strictly speaking, the first 'raising of the flag' but a re-enactment for photographer Jack Rosenthal. The image became a defining image of the US victory in the Pacific, however, there was a lot more fighting to be done even on Iwo Jima, before the Japanese finally surrendered

Suribachi, an extinct volcano that at 550 feet (168 m) is the highest spot on Iwo Jima, to raise a small Stars and Stripes. Two hours later, when the slopes had finally been cleared, a larger flag some 8 feet (2.4 m) long taken from a tank landing ship was raised by five Marines and a navy hospital corpsman. This famous moment was captured by news cameraman Joe Rosenthal, winning him a Pulitzer Prize. Three of the six men in the picture later died on Iwo Jima. A life-size statue of the scene stands as a war memorial in Washington, D.C.

Afterwards the Marines went back to clearing the Japanese out of the tunnels and caves with flamethrowers. Some twenty thousand died in the fighting before the island was secured on 26 March. Some thousand were taken prisoner, while 6,820 Marines were killed and 19,200 wounded.

According to the Iwo Jima Veterans Association, about one third of all Marines killed in action in World War II died on Iwo Jima and twenty-seven Congressional Medals of Honor were awarded for actions on the island.

The next step was Okinawa in the Ryukyu Islands. The battle there began on 26 March 1945 when small islands off Okinawa were seized to act as forward bases in the campaign. The amphibious assault of the main island followed 1 April and fighting lasted until June.

The largest number of ships involved in any Pacific operation – nearly 1,500 – were gathered for the operation and the Allied manpower approached half a million. Although the landings went ahead almost unopposed, kamikaze attacks on the invasion fleet sank twenty-five ships and damaged another 165.

The *Yamato* – the largest battleship ever built – was sent on a one-way mission to

Japanese kamikaze plane burning on the deck of a US aircraft carrier, possibly the USS *Enterprise*, c. May 1945

Wounded Japanese defender on Okinawa emerges from a bunker to surrender to watchful US troops

be beached on Okinawa as a static gun platform. However, with no air cover, she was sunk 200 miles (320 km) short of her destination.

The 77,000 troops of the Thirty-Second Japanese Army, along with the men, women and children of the island's militia, halted the Americans on the Shuri line, named for an ancient castle nearby. At the end of May, the Japanese withdrew to more southerly positions. Still the Americans were held back by fanatical defence and abominable weather conditions. Leaflets urging the defenders to surrender had little effect.

Scorning an American offer of surrender to prevent any further unnecessary loss of life, on 21 June Lieutenant General Mitsuri Ushijima and his Chief of Staff knelt outside their headquarters and committed hara kiri. His final order was that his men should revert to guerrilla warfare. They

continued fighting until the end of the month when some 7,400 gave themselves up, the first time the Japanese had surrendered in large numbers. At least 110,000 Japanese soldiers were dead, and there had been a large number of civilian casualties. For the Allies, it was the costliest operation in the Pacific, with some half a million men involved in the fighting. US ground forces had lost 7,203 killed and 31,807 wounded. The navy had lost some five thousand killed and a similar number wounded.

Japan had lost its entire navy and, during the Battle of Okinawa, 7,800 Japanese aircraft had been destroyed for the loss of 763 Allied planes. The Japanese mainland now lay wide open. It had no defence against the continual bombing raids the USAAF flew against it, and the British and American fleets that surrounded the islands could shell it at will.

Chapter 13
ENDGAME

Marshal Josef Stalin, Prime Minister Winston Churchill and President Truman with staff around the conference table at Potsdam, July 1945

By the spring of 1945 Japan had lost the war of the Pacific. But just as loyal Germans had fought on the streets of Berlin during the dying hours of the Third Reich, so the Japanese reserves would surely battle long and hard to defend the heart of the empire against invaders. Some 5,300 aircraft had been held back on the home islands to carry out kamikaze attacks and some 3,300 suicide boats were being packed with explosives to greet the Allied invasion force.

Nonetheless, plans were prepared for the invasion of the home islands involving as many as five million Allied troops. Operation Olympic, the codename given to an attack on Kyushu, was sched-

uled to begin on 1 October 1945. A second operation known as Coronet would deliver the final blow in the early months of the following year.

The end of the war in Europe would free up plenty of manpower to carry out the task. However, resources were still required by the British fighting in south-east Asia and the Americans fighting on the Philippines.

On 12 April 1945 President Roosevelt died and Harry S. Truman became president. He ordered another review of the invasion plans. The question was asked: With the odds stacked against her, would Japan surrender? Many of her cities were already in ruins thanks to the ceaseless B-29 strategic

The US B-29 bomber which dropped the first atomic bomb on Hiroshima during World War II, now at Roswell Army Airfield in New Mexico

bombing. The submarine blockade had deprived the islands of the raw materials needed to continue the fight. Kamikaze planes would not be able to get off the ground without fuel. Indeed, the army and defiant civilians could not fight without food. Shortages in Japan were already chronic in the early months of 1945. Some top ranking generals believed that capitulation was only a matter of time, even that the estimates of one million Allied casualties had been hopelessly inflated.

Twelve days after taking office, President Truman was briefed about the atomic bomb that had been developed under conditions of great secrecy at Los Alamos, New Mexico. As early as 1904 it had been noted that the decay of radioactive elements gave off a great deal of energy. Physicists then sought to harness this energy. Many of those involved were Jewish and fled the Continent with the rise of Hitler. They began work on an atomic bomb, first in Britain, then in America.

Churchill gave his consent for the bomb to be used against Japan as early as 4 July, before it had even been tested. He later gave his reasons for doing so: 'To avert a vast, indefinite butchery, to bring the war to an end, to give peace to the world, to lay healing hands upon its tortured peoples by a manifestation of overwhelming power at the cost of a few explosions, seemed, after all our toils and perils, the miracle of development.'

The first plutonium bomb detonation occurred at Alamogordo on 16 July 1945. The following day the victors in the European war met in the Berlin suburb of Potsdam. At the conference Truman told Stalin of the existence of the bomb. At this point the Soviet Union had not declared war on Japan and Japanese envoys had made peace overtures via Russian diplomats, but Stalin neglected to say that these came from the highest level.

Dropping Little Boy

Almost before the dust settled from the test, the first uranium bomb, nicknamed 'Little Boy', was being loaded on to the USS *Indianapolis* in San Francisco – a ship that had just undergone repairs to damage caused by a kamikaze at Okinawa. A canister containing the bomb was welded to the deck for the long journey to Tinian. After leaving American shores on 16 July it took ten days to complete the journey to its Pacific destination.

No one on board except for a select few knew

Allied officers look out over the ruins of Hiroshima after the dropping of the atomic bomb

the nature of the cargo. The disaster that might have been soon became starkly apparent. Three days after the bomb was taken off the ship it was torpedoed by a Japanese submarine.

On 6 August Operation Centreboard swung into action. Early in the morning a USAF B-29 called *Enola Gay* bearing the atomic bomb, under the command of Colonel Paul W. Tibbets, took off from Tinian. Some hours later the fearsome weapon, producing a blast equivalent to 20,000 tons of TNT, was unleashed above Hiroshima. Everything in a two-mile radius of the explosion's epicentre was vaporized. The subsequent inferno was so immense that a tail gunner on *Enola Gay*

exclaimed: 'My God, what have we done?'

Another crew member, Sergeant George Caron, described the deadly mushroom cloud he saw forming behind him: 'It's like a mass of bubbling molasses. The mushroom is spreading out. It's maybe a mile or two wide and half a mile high. It's growing up and up. It's nearly level with us and climbing. It's very black but there is a purplish tint to the cloud. The base of the mushroom looks like a heavy undercast that is shot through with flames.'

In an instant the death toll was an estimated 78,000. Thousands more were injured as the shock wave spread across the city, shortly followed by a firestorm and many of those would die from their horrific wounds. The devastating effects of radiation were felt for years to come. A city of ninety-thousand buildings was reduced to just 28,000 while the shape of warfare was changed forever. There was no distinction whatsoever between military and civilian targets. All were swept to their deaths by a deadly nuclear wind, just as the scientists, military and politicians knew they would be.

From the Allied point of view the unconditional surrender they required was still not forthcoming.

The Soviet Union declared war on Japan on 8 August. The following day a second atomic bomb was dropped from a B-29 called Bockscar on Nagasaki, where about 39,000 people were killed. Japan could not sustain any further relentless retribution by the Allies.

The following day, after late night crisis talks in the cabinet, the Japanese accepted surrender terms 'on the understanding that it does not comprise any demand which prejudices the prerogatives of the Emperor as sovereign ruler.'

Signing the documents of surrender aboard the USS *Missouri*, 2 September 1945, ending World War II

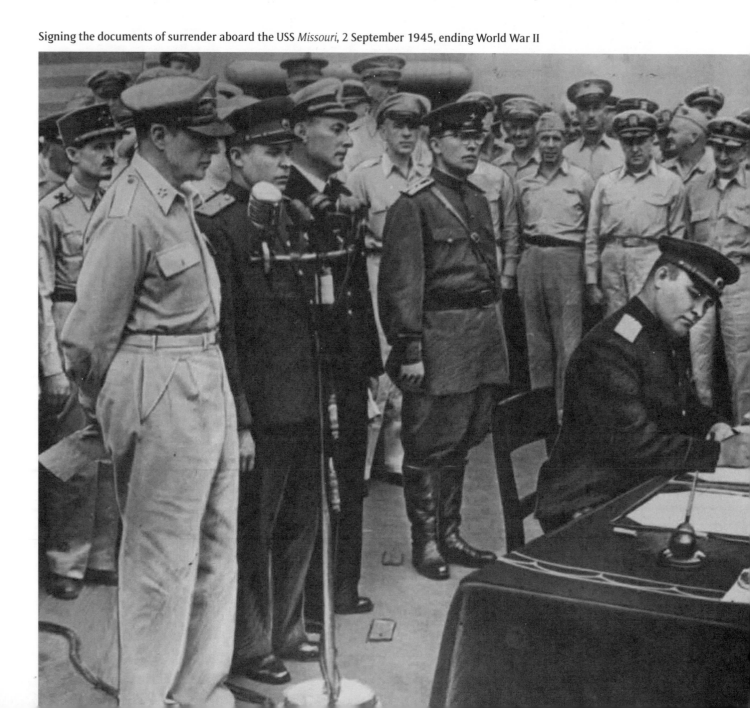

Surrender

Japanese soldiers had gone off to war in 1941 with unrealistically inflated views on their own ability to win. Troops leaving Japan were given a booklet to enlighten them as to the nature of their enemies.

'Westerners,' it said, 'being very superior people, very effeminate and very cowardly – have an intense dislike of fighting in the rain or the mist or at night. Night in particular (although it is excellent for dancing), they cannot conceive to be a proper time for war. In this, if we seize upon it, lies our great opportunity.'

Later, in a pamphlet called 'The Psychology of the Individual American' distributed to Japanese troops they learned more about the Americans: 'They are expert liars, they are taken in by flattery and propaganda. Their desires are very materialistic. They go into battle with no spiritual incentive, and rely on material superiority.'

However, by 1945, the Japanese had learnt a different lesson. Their dream of a vast empire, the Great East Asia Co-Prosperity Sphere, now lay in

tatters. Their navy was not invincible and their army could be beaten despite the tenacity of its soldiers. The Japanese population on the home islands, in prison camps and fighting in the occupied territories bowed their heads when they heard the Emperor broadcast to his subjects on 14 August. It was the first time they had heard his voice.

He told his people they must 'endure the unendurable and suffer the insufferable'. He was not talking about the after effects of the atomic bomb, but of surrender. Even now some in his regime harboured hopes of an honourable defeat and stormed the Emperor's palace in a bid to halt the process of surrender. They were beaten back by the Emperor's loyal guard.

> *On 2 September 1945 Japanese representative Mamoru Shigemitsu, the one-legged foreign minister clad in top hat and tails, signed the surrender on board the battleship USS* Missouri...

VJ (Victory over Japan) day was held on 15 August, with celebrations worldwide. Some of the most heartfelt were among the American citizens of Japanese extraction who had been held behind barbed wire in internment camps since the outbreak of war as a possible threat to national security.

On 2 September 1945 Japanese representative Mamoru Shigemitsu, the one-legged foreign minister clad in top hat and tails, signed the surrender on board the battleship USS *Missouri* in Tokyo Bay. General MacArthur was asked by one of his aides: 'Are you going to call on the Emperor?'

'No,' he replied. 'The Emperor will come to me.'

And a few days later he did. He told MacArthur: 'I come to you... to offer myself to the judgement of the powers you represent as the one who bears sole responsibility for every political and military decision made and action taken by my people in the conduct of the war.'

He was not, however, charged as a war criminal, an issue that would cause controversy for years afterwards. However, it was deemed likely that armed insurrection would occur if the position of Emperor had been compromised.

War Crimes Trials

Winston Churchill was not in favour of the war crimes trials after World War II. He thought the top Nazis should simply be executed. However, at the conference held at Yalta in February 1945, Britain, America and the Soviet Union agreed to prosecute the Nazi leaders and other war criminals.

An International Military Tribunal was set up by the London conference in August 1945. It was given the authority to indict offenders on three counts: crimes against peace – that is, planning and initiating wars of aggression; crimes against humanity – genocide, extermination and deportation; and war crimes – that is, violations of the laws of war. Each of the four Great Powers – Britain, America, the Soviet Union and France – would provide one judge and a prosecutor.

The International Military Tribunal first sat on 18 October 1945, in the Supreme Court Building in Berlin. The first session was presided over by the Soviet member, General Iola T. Nikitschenko. The prosecution entered indictments against twenty-four Nazi leaders and six 'criminal organisations' – Hitler's cabinet, the leadership corps of the Nazi party, the SS (party police) and SD (security police), the Gestapo, the SA (party 'storm troopers') and the General Staff and High Command of the army.

On 20 November 1945, the tribunal moved to the Nuremberg Palace of Justice. This was chosen because it was spacious with about eighty court-rooms and some 530 offices. War damage was minimal and it had a large, undamaged prison attached. The sessions there were held under the presidency of Lord Justice Geoffrey Lawrence (later Baron Trevethin and Oaksey) and procedures followed Anglo-American practice. During the 218 days of the trials, testimony from 360 witnesses was introduced, with 236 witnesses appearing in the court itself.

On 1 October 1946, the verdict was handed down on twenty-two of the original defendants. Slave-labour-organizer Robert Ley had committed suicide in jail and armaments-manufacturer Gustav Krupp von Bohlen und Halbach was too ill to appear in court and the charges against him were dropped.

Hans Frank, the governor-general of Poland; Wilhelm Frick, minister of internal affairs; Alfred Jodl, Hitler's strategic adviser; Ernst Kaltenbrunner, head of the SD; Field Marshal Wilhelm Keitel; Joachim von Ribbentrop, Hitler's foreign minister; Alfred Rosenberg, minister for the occupied territories; Fritz Sauckel, another organizer of forced labour; Julius Streicher, anti-Semitic propagandist and gauleiter in Franconia; and Arthur Seyss-Inquart, commissioner for the occupied Netherlands, were all sentenced to death and hanged in the early morning of 16 October 1946 in the old gymnasium of the Nuremberg prison. The bodies were cremated in Munich and the ashes were strewn in an estuary of the Isar River.

The Reckoning

The head of the Luftwaffe Hermann Göring was also sentenced to death, but committed suicide before he could be executed. And Nazi party organizer Martin Bormann was sentenced to death in absentia, though he was officially declared dead in 1973 after a body identified as his had been unearthed in Berlin.

Walter Funk, minister for economic affairs and president of the German central bank, was sentenced to life imprisonment, but released in 1957 due to illness. He died in 1960. Erich Raeder, commander-in-chief of the navy, got life, but was released in 1955 due to illness and died in 1960. Rudolf Hess, Hitler's deputy who made the dramatic flight to Scotland in 1941, also got life. He committed suicide in 1987 in Spandau prison in Berlin, where the other Nuremberg detainees were held.

Karl Dönitz, admiral of the fleet and Hitler's successor, was sentenced to ten years' imprisonment. He was released in 1956 and died in 1980. Albert Speer, minister for weapons and munitions, was sentenced to twenty years. Released in 1966, he died in 1981. Baldur von Schirach, head of the ministry for youth and gauleiter of Vienna, was also sentenced to twenty years. He was released in 1966 and died in 1974. And Konstantin von Neurath, protector of Bohemia and Moravia, was sentenced to fifteen years' imprisonment. Released in 1954 due to illness, he died in 1956.

Hans Fritzsche, head of the news service section in the ministry of propaganda and essentially a stand-in for Goebbels who had committed suicide, was acquitted, but in the subsequent denazification procedures he was sentenced to nine years' imprisonment. He was released in 1950 and died in 1953. Franz von Papen, vice-chancellor in Hitler's first cabinet was acquitted. In denazification procedures, he was sentenced to eight years' imprisonment. Released in 1949, he died in 1969.

Also acquitted was Horace Greely Hjalmar Schacht, president of the Reichsbank and minister of economics who had been imprisoned in the concentration camp at Flossenbürg since 1944. The German authorities imprisoned him until 1948. He died in 1970.

Guilty verdicts were also handed down on the leadership corps of the NSDAP (Nazi Party), the SS, the SD and the Gestapo.

Although it was originally planned for the International Military Tribunal to sit again, the Cold War had started and there was no further co-operation among the participants. However, more military tribunals sat in the separate French, British, American and Soviet zones of occupation. The US tribunals sat at Nuremberg and on 9 December 1946, proceedings began against twenty-three German doctors who were accused of participating in the Nazi 'euthanasia' programme to murder the mentally deficient and conducting medical experiments on concentration camp inmates.

The trial lasted 140 days. Eighty-five witnesses appeared and 1,500 documents were introduced in evidence. Sixteen of the doctors were found guilty. Seven were sentenced to death and executed on 2 June 1948.

In the twelve subsequent proceedings at Nuremberg, 175 Germans were convicted. In all ten thousand Germans were convicted and 250 sentenced to death.

The Potsdam declaration of July 1945 also called for trial of those who had 'deceived and misled' the Japanese people into war. As commander of the occupation General Douglas MacArthur arrested thirty-nine suspects, most of them members of

General Tojo's war cabinet. The shame of being branded a war criminal cut deep for numerous Japanese leaders, many whom chose to commit suicide. Tojo himself tried to commit suicide, but was resuscitated by American doctors.

Trials and Tribulations

In Manila, MacArthur had already held war crimes trials that had resulted in the execution of Generals Yamashita and Homma and there were doubts about the legitimacy of such proceedings. Nevertheless, on 6 October MacArthur was given the authority to try suspects under three broad categories. Class A charges alleging 'crimes against peace' were to be brought against Japan's top leaders who had planned and directed the war. Class B and C charges, which could be levelled at Japanese of any rank, covered 'conventional war crimes' and 'crimes against humanity', respectively. And in early November, MacArthur was also given authority to purge other war-time leaders from public life.

On 19 January 1946, the International Military Tribunal for the Far East was established with eleven judges. Sir William Webb, an Australian, was the tribunal's president and US assistant attorney general Joseph Keenan was chief prosecutor.

The Tokyo trials began on 3 May 1946, and lasted two-and-a-half years. On 4 November 1948, all of the remaining defendants had been found guilty. Seven were sentenced to death, sixteen to life terms and two to lesser terms. Two had died during the trials and one had been found insane. After reviewing their decisions, MacArthur praised the work of the tribunal and upheld the verdicts. Nevertheless Tojo continued to protest his innocence.

'Never at any time did I conceive that the waging of this war would or could be challenged by the

victors as an international crime,' he said, 'or that regularly constituted officials of the vanquished nations would be charged individually as criminals under any recognized international law or under alleged violations of treaties between nations. I feel that I did no wrong. I feel that I did what was right and true.'

Atonement

On 23 December 1948, General Tojo and six others were hanged at Sugamo prison. Afraid of antagonizing the Japanese people, MacArthur defied the wishes of President Truman and banned photography. Instead four members of the Allied Council were present as official witnesses.

The Tokyo trials were not the only forum for the punishment of Japanese war criminals. The Asian countries that had suffered under the Japanese war machine tried an estimated five-thousand suspected war criminals, executing as many as nine hundred and sentencing more than half to life in prison.

At the time, the Japanese were thought to be brutal fighters, guilty of shocking savagery. They were capable of beating sick and wounded men and disembowelling women and children. Famously they beheaded prisoners of war with one swing of a sword. However, most Japanese soldiers fought in the same manner as other soldiers around the globe during the era and many passed the dull hours between action writing Tanka, traditional five line poems that were both lyrical and moving.

Intelligence reports based on interrogation of prisoners captured during Allied attacks on Japanese-held islands in early May 1945 revealed still more about the serving soldiers, most of whom were conscripted men.

The reports suggest that, rather than being ruthless fanatics, morale was generally low among Japanese troops, particularly the conscripts. Most draftees were aging, ill-equipped and in poor health. With barely a month's training, they were no match for the advancing Allies. They appeared to particularly resent the superior attitude and arrogance of regular Japanese soldiers, NCOs and officers.

The Japanese were thought to be brutal fighters, capable of shocking savagery. However, most Japanese soldiers fought in the same manner as other soldiers around the globe during the era...

Prisoner PW X3004 Konno Kleichi, a thirty-year-old farmer captured north of Omanay on 2 May 1945, had been unable to keep up with his unit's retreat – hardly surprising given the debilitating effects of malaria. The interrogating officer, Squadron Leader F. W. Clifton of the Royal Australian Air Force, noted that: 'Morale of troops in PW's unit was very low. All of the 120 men in the unit, except three or four, were ill at various times with malaria. CO of the Unit, 1st Lieutenant Togashi, addressed the men on 29th April 1945 and told them that there was nothing left for them to do but swallow their pride and retreat.'

Under 'remarks' Clifton added: 'PW had received little military training and had not fired his rifle on this island.'

Another of Clifton's interviewees, PW X2011 Sadayoshi Tenga, a thirty-year-old fish market owner serving as a Private First Class with the 165th II Battalion, 75th Bdo, was captured on Samal island on 8 May. He said he had deserted to anti-Japanese guerrilla forces because he was 'disgusted with ill treatment received from army officers and NCOs'. Tenga believed that, for the same reason, many conscripts had deserted on Mindanao and had 'gone to the mountains'. He told Clifton: 'The attitude of the regular soldiers to the newly-conscripted men was that of contempt. PW was often ill-treated by officers and men.'

Tying Up the Loose Ends

Another interrogation report reveals the nobility of one Major Matsuzaki in the Philippines when dealing with a young woman with a Japanese father and the Filipina mother who had been found guilty of spying for the Americans. Clearly, they had previously developed a father-daughter relationship that came into play when the convicted woman requested that the major carried out her execution. The date was deferred by a day as it was the Emperor's birthday and, that night, the major negotiated her escape to Samal Island. She survived to be interrogated closely by a squadron leader in the Royal Australian Air Force in May 1945. The fate of the major is unknown.

On 10 September 1945 Briton R. Munby was posted to Singapore to help oversee the transition of power from the vanquished to the victors. Shortly before his arrival 300 Japanese officers committed hari kiri or ritual suicide in the lounge of the Raffles Hotel. A whole platoon of officers also blew themselves up with hand grenades.

'The Chinese in Chinatown were much happier to see the British than the Malayans,' Munby noted. 'Everywhere there I was met with pleasant faces and words of thanks though many of the poorer people were so near to starvation point that it must have been indeed an effort for them even to smile. The very fact that I saw a dead woman dressed in the black smock of the working class, lying in the gutter, most conspicuous but completely unheeded by passers-by pointed conclusively to the fact that such bodies were a common sight during the Japanese reign of terror.'

He watched as Japanese prisoners were marched to the YMCA building – previously the headquarters of the Kempei, the notorious Japanese secret police.

'The Japs passed within three feet of where I was standing and it was interesting to note the expressions on their faces,' said Munby. 'Some showed signs of great humiliation and were probably unwilling tools forced to carry out their government's orders; others were arrogant, brutal creatures to whom the catcalls and derision of the crowd meant not a thing.'

Last Man Standing

One of Japan's war aims was achieved. They had demonstrated that Britain and the other European powers were unable to protect the indigenous population as promised and, in the decades following the war, withdrew from their colonies. But while Japan gave up militarism and turned itself into an industrial power, some Imperial soldiers fought on. On 9 March 1974, Second Lieutenant Hiroo Onada emerged from the jungle of Lubang Island in the Philippines still armed with a rifle and hand grenades, one of numerous soldiers who refused to believe the fight had finished. Onada was duly relieved of military duty. He did not surrender. Only private Teruo Nakamura, a native Taiwanese arrested in Indonesia on 18 December 1974, held out longer.

Crowds gathering in Times Square to read the news of Japan's surrender on V-J (Victory Japan) Day, New York City

INDEX

Aachen 109
Adderley, Herbert 157
Akyab airfield 150
Albania 34
Aleutian Islands 73, 76, 160–1
Alexander, Sir Harold 41, 48–9, 84, 86
Alexandria 39
Algeria 46
Algiers 46
Anderson, Kenneth 46, 47
Angerapp River 122
Anti-Comintern Pact 15
Antwerp 111
Anzio 84–5
Arakan 150
Archangel 53
Ardennes 23, 111–14
Arnhem 109–11
Arnim Hans-Jürgen 47–9
Arrras 25
Auchinleck, Claude 39, 41, 140
Augusta 81
Auschwitz 57, 58, 124–5, 125
Austria 12
Australia 140
Babi Yar 52
Bari 83
Bastogne 112
Bataan Peninsula 139
Battle of Britain 28–32, 34
Beck, Josef 15
Belgium 22–3, 25, 109, 111
Bolgorod 106
Belorussia 55
Benes, Edvard 12, 14
Bergen concentration camp 120–2
Berlin 32, 129–33, 135
Betio Island 161, 162
Bielski Otriad 58
Bizerte 46, 49
Blitz, The 32, 34
Blitzkrieg 11, 19
Blumentritt, Günther 15
Bock, Fedor von 51, 56
Bologna 82
Bône 46–7
Bormann, Martin 132, 185
Borneo 139
Bose, Chandra 155
Boulogne 25
Bourguebus Ridge 99
Bradley, Omar 49, 99, 100
Braun, Eva 132
Brest 26
Brindisi 82
Brotheridge, Herbert Denham 91
Bryansk 56
Budapest 124, 124
Bulgaria 103
Bulge, Battle of the 111–14
Burma 140, 150–8
Busse, Theodor 129, 130
Caen 95, 96–7, 99
Calabria 82
Calais 25, 92
Canal d'Aire 25
Caron, George 181

Casablanca 46
Catania 81
Chamberlain, Neville 12–13, 13, 14, 20, 22
Cherbourg 26, 95, 96, 98
China
    casualties 6
    destruction in 7
    rise of Communist Party 7
    threat from Japan 67–8
Chindits, The 151–4
Choltitz, Dietrich von 102
Chuikov, Vasili 60–1, 63
Churchill, Winston 179
    on German rearmament 14
    and invasion of Norway 20
    becomes Prime Minister 22
    gives 'Battle of Britain' speech 28
    orders bombing of Berlin 32
    gives 'Never in the field of human conflict' speech 32
    and fall of Tobruk 39
    sacks Auchinleck 41
    on battle of El Alamein 46
    on invasion of Italy 84
    and opening of second front 89
    on the Chindits 152–3
    view of war crimes trials 184
Clark, Mark 82, 86, 87
Clifton, F. W. 187
Compiègne 27
Coral Sea, Battle of the 72, 147
Corregidor 139
Cotentin Peninsula 96
Crerar, Henry 99
Crete 33, 34
Currie, John 45
Czechoslovakia 12–15
D-Day 89–95
Danzig 15
de Gaulle, Charles 27, 102
Denmark 20
Dieppe 89
Dietrich, Sepp 111, 113
Dollfuss, Engelbert 12
Donahue, James 141, 142, 143, 146–7
Donitz, Karl 132, 185
Doolittle Raid 71–2
Dresden 116, 117
Dunkirk 25–6
Dvinsk 52
Dyle, Rover 23
Eastern Solomons, Battle of the 144
Eben Emael 22
Egypt 36
Eisenhower, Dwight D.
    and Operation Torch 46
    and Operation Strike 49
    and D-Day 90
    and Falaise Gap 102
    and Battle of the Bulge 112
    and bombing of Germany 114
    orders halt of Allied forces 130
El Agheila 36, 38
El Alamein 36, 39–46
El Guettar 49
Elbe River 130
Endifaville 49
Enna 81
Ethiopia 10

Europe
    effects of World War II 7
Falaise Gap 99–100, 102
Far East
    Japanese advance through 137–40
    Burma 150–8
    assault on India 154–8
Final Solution 52, 57–8, 120–2
Finland 53
Fletcher, Jack 140, 144
Fondouk 49
France
    declares war on Germany 18
    and invasion of Poland 19
    military strength of 21
    invasion of 23, 23–7
    and D-Day 89–95
    and the Bocage 95–6
    breakout from Caen 99
    and Falaise Gap 99–100, 102
    liberation of Paris 102–3
Frank, Hans 185
Fredendall, Lloyd R. 46
Freyberg, Bernard 85
Frick, Wilhelm 185
Fritzsche, Hans 185
Fuchida, Mitsui 69–70, 140
Funk, Walter 185
Gafsa 48
Galland, Adolf 117
Gatehouse, Alec 43, 45
Gazala 38–9
Gela 81
Germany
    after Treaty of Versailles 6, 10
    casualties 6, 7
    and rearmament programme 10–11, 13
    non-aggression pact with Soviet Union 15, 51
    Allies enter 109
    bombing campaign in 114, 117
    Allies cross Rhine 119–20
    Soviet troops enter 125–7
    and fall of Berlin 129–33
    surrender of 133, 134
Gilbert Islands 161–2
Goebbels, Joseph 122, 131, 132
Gold Beach 93
Göring, Hermann 10
    and Dunkirk 25
    and Battle of Britain 31
    and Siege of Stalingrad 63
    commits suicide 185
Gort, Viscount 24
Gothic Line 86
Great Britain
    casualties 7
    declares war on Germany 18
    and invasion of Poland 19
    withdrawal from France 25–7
    military strength of 28
    and Battle of Britain 28–32, 34
    support for Soviet Union 53
    declares war on Japan 71
Greece 34
Grynszpan, Herschel 14
Guadalcanal 140–7
Guam 163, 165–6

Guderian, Heinz 11, 129
    and Operation Barbarossa 57
    attempts to stabilize Eastern
Front 122–3, 124, 125, 126–8
Gustav Line 84, 86
Guzzoni, Alfredi 81
Haakon VII, King 22
Hácha, Emil 14
Halsey, William 'Bull' 146, 168
Harman, John 156
Harris, Arthur 114
Heinrici, Gotthard 129, 130
Henderson Field 141, 144
Henlein, Konrad 12
Hess, Rudolf 185
Hill 122 99
Hill 609 49
Hilpert, C. 133
Himmler, Heinrich 126, 129, 132
Hiroshima 181–2
Hitler, Adolf 11, 13, 101, 133
    influenced by Mussolini 6
    political ideas of 9
    starts rearmament programme 10–11
    and occupation of Rhineland 11
    and occupation of Austria 12
    and occupation of Czechoslovakia 12–14
    and invasion of Poland 15
    orders halt in invasion of France 25–6
    signs 'Pact of Steel' 27
    at French armistice 27
    and Operation Sealion 28, 32
    orders bombing of London 32
    orders invasion of Crete 34
    orders Rommel not to withdraw 45
    and Operation Barbarossa 51, 56
    and Siege of Stalingrad 59, 60, 63, 64
    declares war on United States 71
    reaction to D-Day 95
    belief in V rockets 97
    and Falaise Gap 99–100
    orders destruction of Paris 102
    and Battle of Kursk 105, 107
    assassination attempt in 108
    and Battle of the Bulge 111
    orders scorched earth policy 119
    and Soviet advance through E Europe 122–4, 126, 128, 129
    returns to Berlin 125
    during fall of Berlin 130, 132
    commits suicide 132
Hollis, Stan 93
Homma, Masaharu 186
Hong Kong 138
Horrocks, Brian 109
Hoth, Hermann 57
Howard, John 91
Hube, Hans 81, 82
Hungary 125, 128
Imita Ridge 147
Imphal 152, 155–8
India 7, 154–8

Inui, Genjirous 144–6
Italy
    rise of Benito Mussolini 6
    invasion of France 27
    military strength of 78
    plans for invasion of 78–9
    invasion of Sicily 78–82
    starts negotiations with Allies 82
    invasion of mainland 82–6
    Iwo Jima 173–6
Japan
    after Treaty of Versailles 6
    casualties 7
    colonial ambitions of 66–8
    Doolittle Raid on 71–2
    bombing of 166, 179–80
    use of atomic bombs on 180–2
    surrender 182–4
Java Sea, Battle of the 139–40
Jews
    persecution starts 10
    and Kristallnacht 14
    persecution after invasion of Poland 20
    start of Final Solution 52
    Final Solution planned 57–8
    resistance 58
    liberation of concentration camps 120–2
    on 'death marches' 125
Jodl, Alfred 185
Joyce, William 37
Juno Beach 93
Kaku, Captain 76
'kamikaze' attacks 170–2
Kasserine Pass 48
Kato, Masuo 166
Keenan, Joseph 186
Keiji, Shibasaki 161
Keitel, Wilhelm 185
Kerch Peninsula 59
Kesselring, Albert 47, 85
    and invasion of Italy 81, 82, 83, 84, 86
Kharkov 59. 107
Kidney Ridge 43
Kiev 52, 55
Kincaid, Thomas 161
Kleichi, Konno 187
Kluge, Gunther von 97, 99–100, 102
Kobe 166
Kohima 155–8
Kokoda 147, 148
Konev, Ivan 129–30, 132
Kramer, Josef 121
Kristallnacht 14
Krupp von Buhlen und Halbach, Gustav 185
Kuala Lumpur 137
Kurile Islands 69
Kurita, Takeo 167, 168
Kursk, Battle of 105–7
Küstrin River 129
Lake Ladoga 53
Lambert, Harold 154
Lammerding, Heinz 127
Lary, Virgil 112–13
Latvia 52
Lawrence, Geoffrey 185
Le Mans 100
Le May, Curtis 166

League of Air Sports 11
League of Nations 10
Leeb, Wilhelm von 51
Leningrad 52–3
Leopold, King 25
Leuna fuel works 117
Ley, Robert 185
Leyte Gulf, Battle of 167–8, 170
Liège 24
Linggayen Gulf 139
Liri Valley 85, 86
Lithuania 52
Locarno Pact 11
Longstop Hill 47
Lucas, John P. 84
Lumsden, Herbert 43
Luxembourg 23
Luzon 170, 172–3
MacArthur, Douglas 167, 184, 186, 187
Maginot Line 21, 22, 27
Maizila Pass 48
Makin 161
Malaya 137
Malmédy massacre 112–13
Mamayev Hill 61
Manila 139, 173
Manstein, Erich von 15, 63–4
Manteuffel, Hasso von 129
Marcinkonis 58
Mareth Line 48, 49
Marianas Islands 163–4
Marshall Islands 162–3
Mateur 49
Matsuzaki, Major 188
McAuliffe, Anthony 112
Medenine 48
Mers-el-Kébir 27–8
Mersa Matruh 39
Messina 81, 82
Metzger, Lothar 117
Meuse, River 24
Meyer, Lawrence C. 144
Michael I, King 103
Midway, Battle of 73–6
Mikawa, Gunichi 144
Milan 86
Milne Bay 147–8
Miteiriya Ridge 43
Mitscher, Marc 165
Model, Walther 105, 122
Molotov, Vyacheslav 51
Molotov-Ribbentrop Pact 15, 51
Montagu, Ewen 78
Monte Cassino 84, 85–6
Montgomery, Bernard 40
    at battle of El Alamein 41, 42–3, 44–5
    and Operation Torch 48, 49
    and invasion of Sicily 79, 81
    and invasion of Italy 83
    and breakout from Caen 99
    and Arhhem 108
    and crossing of the Rhine 119
    and surrender of Germany 135
Morocco 46
Morshead, Leslie 36
Mortain 100
Moscow 56–7
Mount Etna 81
Mulberry harbours 98–9

Munby, R. 188
Murphy, M. P. 151
Mussolini, Benito 11, 78–9, 101
    rise of 6
    invades Ethiopia 10
    signs 'Pact of Steel' 27
    orders attack on Egypt 36
    arrested and imprisoned 84
    rescued from prison 82
    killed 86
Mutaguchi, Renya 154, 155
Nagasaki 182
Nagumo, Chuichi 69, 70
Nakamura, Teruo 188
Narvik 20
Netherlands 21–2, 109–11
Nettuno 84
Neurath, Konstantin von 185
Nikitschenko, Iola 184
Nikulina, Anna 132–3
Nimitz, Chester 71
Nishimura, Shoji 168
Noak, General 133
Nomonhan, Battle of 67
North Africa
    Italian attack in 36
    battles on El Alamein 36, 39–46
    Siege of Tobruk 36–8
    advance on Gazala 38–9
    and Operation Torch 46–9
Norway 20–1, 133, 134
O'Connor, Richard 36
Okinawa 173, 176–7
Olver, Hartley 120–1
Omaha Beach 92–3, 94–5
Onada, Hiroo 188
Onishi, Takijirio 170, 172
Operation Barbarossa 51–7
Operation Dynamo 25–6
Operation Flintlock 162–3
Operation Fortitude 89
Operation Galvanic 161–2
Operation Goodwood 99
Operation Husky 79–82
Operation Market Garden 109–11
Operation Mincemeat 78–9
Operation Overlord 89–95
Operation Saar 19
Operation Sealion 28–32
Operation Strike 49
Operation Supercharge 44–5
Operation Torch 46–9
Operation Zitadelle 105
Oran 46
Orel salient 106
Orne Rover 99
Ozawa, Jizaburo 164, 167
Pacific War
    attack on Pearl Harbor 67, 68–70
    Battle of the Coral Sea 72
    Battle of Midway 73–6
    attack on Guadalcanal 140–7
    Battle of the Eastern Solomons 144
    Battle of Santa Cruz 147
    and Aleutian Islands 160–1
    and Operation Galvanic 161–2
    and Marianas Islands 163–4
    and Okinawa 173, 176–7

    and Iwo Jima 173–6
Pact of Steel 27, 34
Palau Islands 167
Palermo 81
Papen, Franz von 185–6
Papua New Guinea 140, 147–8
Paris 102–3
Pas de Calais 91
Patton, George S.
    and Operation Torch 46, 48, 49
    and invasion of Sicily 79, 81
    and D-Day 89
    and breakout from Caen 99
    and Falaise Gap 100, 102
    and crossing of the Rhine 119
Paulus, Friedrich 60, 63, 64
Pavesi, Gino 79
Pearl Harbor 67, 68–70
Pegasus Bridge 91–2
Peiper, Joachim 112, 113
Peleliu 167
Percival, Arthur 138
Petacci, Claretta 86
Pétain, Philippe 27
Philippine Sea, Battle of the 164–5
Philippines 139, 167, 172–3
'Phoney War' 20
Poland
    casualties 7
    non-aggression pact with Germany 10
    preparations for invasion 15
    invasion of 18–20
    Soviet advance through 108–9
Port Moresby 147, 148
Potsdam conference 179
Primsole 80
Prikhorovka 106
Qattara Depression 39–40
Quisling, Vidkun 20
Rabaul 147, 160
Raeder, Erich 29, 185
Ramsay, Bertram 25
Ramsey, Logan 70
Randle, John 158
Rauss, Erhard 128–9
Rees, Taffy 156–7
Remagen 119
Reynaud, Paul 27
Rhine River 119–20
Rhineland 11
Ribbentrop, Joachim von 18, 51, 185
Riga 52
Ritchie, Neil 39
Rochefort, Joseph P. 73
Rokossovsky, Konstantin 130
Romania 34, 103
Rome 82, 83, 84, 86
Rommel, Erwin 44
    and invasion of France 27
    and Siege of Tobruk 36–7
    and advance on Gazala 38–9
    and battles at El Alamein 39, 40, 41, 42–3, 44, 45
    and Operation Torch 48, 49
    and invasion of Italy 82, 83–4
    and D-Day 90
    and Caen 96–7
    in plot to kill Hitler 99
Roosevelt, Franklin D. 41, 70–1, 179

INDEX

Rosenberg, Alfred 185
Rosenthal, Jack 175, 176
Rundstedt, Gerd von
    and invasion of Poland 15
    and invasion of France 23
    and Operation Sealion 29
    and Operation Barbarossa 51
    and Caen 96–7
Ryder, Charles 46
Saint-Malo 26
St Mere Eglise 91
Saint-Nazaire 26–7
Saipan 163–4
Salerno 82–3
San Bernardino Strait 168
Sangro River 84
Santa Cruz, Battle of 147
Santo Stefano 81
Sato, Kotoku 158
Sauckel, Fritz 185
Schacht, Horace 186
Schindler, Oskar 58
Schirach, Baldur von 185
Schmidt, Paul 13
Schmundt, Rudolf 15
Schörner, Ferdinand 129
Schuschnigg, Kurt von 12
Sedan, Rover 24
Seine, River 27
Seyss-Inquart, Arthur 12, 185
Shaw, Ted 109–10, 121–2
Shigemitsu, Mamoru 184
Sibuyan Sea, Battle of the 167–8
Sicily 78–82
Sidi Barrani 36
Sidi Bou Zid 46

Sidi Omar 39
Siegfried Line 19
Simpson, William 130
Singapore 137–8
Skorzeny, Otto 82
Slim, William 140, 150
Smolensk 55
Sohibor 58
Sollum 36, 39
Soviet Union
    casualties 6, 7
    non-aggression pact with
    Germany 15, 51
    invasion of Poland 19–20
    and Operation Barbarossa 51–7
    and Siege of Stalingrad 58–64
    advance through Eastern Europe
    122–5
Spaatz, Carl 'Tooey' 114, 133
Spain 11
Speer, Albert 127, 185
Spruance, Raymond 164
Stalin, Joseph 179
    purge of Red Army 15
    reaction to German invasion
    51–3
    and attack on Kiev 55
    remains in Moscow 56
    and Siege of Stalingrad 58–9,
    60
    and Battle of Nomonhan 67
    and attack on Berlin 129–30
Stalingrad 58–64
Streicher, Julius 185
Sudetenland 12–14
Sweden 20
Sword Beach 93
Syracuse 81
Tansley, Ron 121
Taranto 82

Tassigny, Jean de Lattre de Tassigny 135
Tatchell, Rodney 154
Tedder, Sir Arthur 133
Tenga, Sadayoshi 187–8
Termoli 83
Thailand 138
Thoma, Wilhelm von 45
Tibbets, Paul 181
Timmermann, Karl 119
Tobruk 34, 36–8, 39, 40
Tojo, Hideki 186–7
Tokyo 71, 166
Toulon 46
Tripoli 36, 48
Treaty of Versailles 6, 10
Trebble, Hugh 151
Treblinka 58
Truman, Harry S. 179, 180
Tuczyn 58
Tunis 46–7
Tunisia 46–9
Turkey 38
Ukraine 52, 54–5
United States
    casualties 7
    Operation Torch 46
    support for Soviet Union 53
    attack on Pearl Harbor 67,
    68–70
    negotiations with Japan 67–8
Ushijima, Mitsuri 177
Utah Beach 94
V rockets 97
Vichy France
    creation of 27–8
    in North Africa 46
    Allied landings in 102
Vistula River 125
Volga River 58, 60–1, 63
Volturno River 83

Vyazma 56
Wake Island 139
Wallenburg, Raoul 58
Wansee 57
war crime trials 184–7
Ward, Orlando 49
Warsaw 20, 58, 108–9
Wavell, Sir Archibald 36, 140
Webb, Sir William 186
Weichs, Freiherr von 126
Weidling, Helmuth 132
Wenck, Walther 128, 130
Weygand, Maxime 26, 27
Wilhelmina, Queen 22
Wingate, Orde 151, 152, 153
World War I 6
World War II
    origins in World War I 6
    casualties in 6–7
    effects on Europe 7
    events leading to 9–15
Yalta conference 135
Yamaguchi, Tamon 75
Yamashita, Tomoyuki 138, 170, 186
Yamamoto, Isoroku
    and attack on Pearl Harbor 68–9
    and Battle of Midway 72, 73, 76
Yugoslavia 7, 34
Zhukov, Georgii
    and defence of Moscow 56, 57
    and Siege of Stalingrad 61, 63
    and attack on Berlin 129–30,
    132
    and surrender of Germany 133,
    135
Zilch, Gerhard 131–2

PICTURE CREDITS

Getty: 7, 19, 20, 21, 22, 24, 25, 26, 29, 30, 33, 37, 38, 42, 47, 53, 54, 55, 56, 58-9, 62, 64, 67, 80, 86, 92-3, 123, 128, 164, 171 (t), 174, 176, 180, 189

Corbis: 8, 12, 13, 14, 16, 18, 40, 44, 78, 83, 84-5, 107, 127, 134

Imperial War Museum: 152, 155, 156, 161, 162 (b), 171 (b), 172, 175, 177, 179, 181

US Naval Historical Foundation: 68, 72, 73, 74-5, 76, 137, 142, 143, 145, 165, 168-9, 170

Topfoto: 91, 95, 98, 110, 112, 119

US National Archive: 9, 11, 166

Popperfoto: 94

ED Archives: 120

Mary Evans: 10, 105

Bundesarchiv: 52

Shutterstock: 124-5

ITN Archive: 148, 162 (t)